OECD/G20 Base Erosion and Profit Shifting Project

Countering Harmful Tax Practices More Effectively, Taking into Account Transparency and Substance, Action 5 - 2015 Final Report

This document and any map included herein are without prejudice to the status of or sovereignty over any territory, to the delimitation of international frontiers and boundaries and to the name of any territory, city or area.

Please cite this publication as:
OECD (2015), *Countering Harmful Tax Practices More Effectively, Taking into Account Transparency and Substance, Action 5 - 2015 Final Report*, OECD/G20 Base Erosion and Profit Shifting Project, OECD Publishing, Paris.
http://dx.doi.org/10.1787/9789264241190-en

ISBN 978-92-64-24118-3 (print)
ISBN 978-92-64-24119-0 (PDF)

Series: OECD/G20 Base Erosion and Profit Shifting Project
ISSN 2313-2604 (print)
ISSN 2313-2612 (online)

Photo credits: Cover © ninog – Fotolia.com

Corrigenda to OECD publications may be found on line at: *www.oecd.org/about/publishing/corrigenda.htm*.

© OECD 2015

You can copy, download or print OECD content for your own use, and you can include excerpts from OECD publications, databases and multimedia products in your own documents, presentations, blogs, websites and teaching materials, provided that suitable acknowledgement of OECD as source and copyright owner is given. All requests for public or commercial use and translation rights should be submitted to *rights@oecd.org*. Requests for permission to photocopy portions of this material for public or commercial use shall be addressed directly to the Copyright Clearance Center (CCC) at *info@copyright.com* or the Centre français d'exploitation du droit de copie (CFC) at *contact@cfcopies.com*.

Foreword

International tax issues have never been as high on the political agenda as they are today. The integration of national economies and markets has increased substantially in recent years, putting a strain on the international tax rules, which were designed more than a century ago. Weaknesses in the current rules create opportunities for base erosion and profit shifting (BEPS), requiring bold moves by policy makers to restore confidence in the system and ensure that profits are taxed where economic activities take place and value is created.

Following the release of the report *Addressing Base Erosion and Profit Shifting* in February 2013, OECD and G20 countries adopted a 15-point Action Plan to address BEPS in September 2013. The Action Plan identified 15 actions along three key pillars: introducing coherence in the domestic rules that affect cross-border activities, reinforcing substance requirements in the existing international standards, and improving transparency as well as certainty.

Since then, all G20 and OECD countries have worked on an equal footing and the European Commission also provided its views throughout the BEPS project. Developing countries have been engaged extensively via a number of different mechanisms, including direct participation in the Committee on Fiscal Affairs. In addition, regional tax organisations such as the African Tax Administration Forum, the *Centre de rencontre des administrations fiscales* and the *Centro Interamericano de Administraciones Tributarias*, joined international organisations such as the International Monetary Fund, the World Bank and the United Nations, in contributing to the work. Stakeholders have been consulted at length: in total, the BEPS project received more than 1 400 submissions from industry, advisers, NGOs and academics. Fourteen public consultations were held, streamed live on line, as were webcasts where the OECD Secretariat periodically updated the public and answered questions.

After two years of work, the 15 actions have now been completed. All the different outputs, including those delivered in an interim form in 2014, have been consolidated into a comprehensive package. The BEPS package of measures represents the first substantial renovation of the international tax rules in almost a century. Once the new measures become applicable, it is expected that profits will be reported where the economic activities that generate them are carried out and where value is created. BEPS planning strategies that rely on outdated rules or on poorly co-ordinated domestic measures will be rendered ineffective.

Implementation therefore becomes key at this stage. The BEPS package is designed to be implemented via changes in domestic law and practices, and via treaty provisions, with negotiations for a multilateral instrument under way and expected to be finalised in 2016. OECD and G20 countries have also agreed to continue to work together to ensure a consistent and co-ordinated implementation of the BEPS recommendations. Globalisation requires that global solutions and a global dialogue be established which go beyond OECD and G20 countries. To further this objective, in 2016 OECD and G20 countries will conceive an inclusive framework for monitoring, with all interested countries participating on an equal footing.

A better understanding of how the BEPS recommendations are implemented in practice could reduce misunderstandings and disputes between governments. Greater focus on implementation and tax administration should therefore be mutually beneficial to governments and business. Proposed improvements to data and analysis will help support ongoing evaluation of the quantitative impact of BEPS, as well as evaluating the impact of the countermeasures developed under the BEPS Project.

Table of contents

Tables

Abbreviations and acronyms

AOA	Authorised OECD approach
APA	Advance pricing arrangement
ATR	Advance tax ruling
BEPS	Base erosion and profit shifting
CAN	Consolidated application note
CFA	Committee on Fiscal Affairs
CFC	Controlled foreign company
CRS	Common Reporting Standard (Standard for Automatic Exchange of Financial Account Information)
EOI	Exchange of information
EU	European Union
FATF	Financial Action Task Force
FHTP	Forum on Harmful Tax Practices
IP	Intellectual property
MAC	Convention on Mutual Administrative Assistance in Tax Matters
MNE	Multinational enterprise
OECD	Organisation for Economic Co-operation and Development
PE	Permanent establishment
R&D	Research and development
TIN	Taxpayer identification number
TP	Transfer pricing

Executive summary

More than 15 years have passed since the publication of the Organisation for Economic Co-operation and Development's (OECD) 1998 Report *Harmful Tax Competition: An Emerging Global Issue* and the underlying policy concerns expressed then are as relevant today as they were then. Current concerns are primarily about preferential regimes that risk being used for artificial profit shifting and about a lack of transparency in connection with certain rulings. The continued importance of the work on harmful tax practices was highlighted by the inclusion of this work in the *Action Plan on Base Erosion and Profit Shifting* (BEPS Action Plan, OECD, 2013), whose Action 5 committed the Forum on Harmful Tax Practices (FHTP) to:

> *Revamp the work on harmful tax practices with a priority on improving transparency, including compulsory spontaneous exchange on rulings related to preferential regimes, and on requiring substantial activity for any preferential regime. It will take a holistic approach to evaluate preferential tax regimes in the BEPS context. It will engage with non-OECD members on the basis of the existing framework and consider revisions or additions to the existing framework.*

In 2014, the FHTP delivered an initial progress report, which is incorporated into and superseded by this final report. The main focus of the FHTP's work has been on agreeing and applying a methodology to define the substantial activity requirement to assess preferential regimes, looking first at intellectual property (IP) regimes and then other preferential regimes. The work has also focused on improving transparency through the compulsory spontaneous exchange of certain rulings that could give rise to BEPS concerns in the absence of such exchanges.

Requiring substantial activity for preferential regimes

Countries agreed that the substantial activity requirement used to assess preferential regimes should be strengthened in order to realign taxation of profits with the substantial activities that generate them. Several approaches were considered and consensus was reached on the "nexus approach". This approach was developed in the context of IP regimes, and it allows a taxpayer to benefit from an IP regime only to the extent that the taxpayer itself incurred qualifying research and development (R&D) expenditures that gave rise to the IP income. The nexus approach uses expenditure as a proxy for activity and builds on the principle that, because IP regimes are designed to encourage R&D activities and to foster growth and employment, a substantial activity requirement should ensure that taxpayers benefiting from these regimes did in fact engage in such activities and did incur actual expenditures on such activities. This same principle can also be applied to other preferential regimes so that such regimes would be found to require substantial activities where they grant benefits to a taxpayer to the extent that the taxpayer undertook the core income-generating activities required to produce the type of income covered by the preferential regime.

Improving transparency

In the area of transparency, a framework covering all rulings that could give rise to BEPS concerns in the absence of compulsory spontaneous exchange has been agreed. The framework covers six categories of rulings: (i) rulings related to preferential regimes; (ii) cross border unilateral advance pricing arrangements (APAs) or other unilateral transfer pricing rulings; (iii) rulings giving a downward adjustment to profits; (iv) permanent establishment (PE) rulings; (v) conduit rulings; and (vi) any other type of ruling where the FHTP agrees in the future that the absence of exchange would give rise to BEPS concerns. This does not mean that such rulings are *per se* preferential or that they will in themselves give rise to BEPS, but it does acknowledge that a lack of transparency in the operation of a regime or administrative process can give rise to mismatches in tax treatment and instances of double non-taxation. For countries which have the necessary legal basis, exchange of information under this framework will take place from 1 April 2016 for future rulings and the exchange of certain past rulings will need to be completed by 31 December 2016. The Report also sets out best practices for cross-border rulings.

Review of preferential regimes

A total of 43 preferential regimes have been reviewed, out of which 16 are IP regimes. The Report contains the results of the application of the existing factors in the 1998 Report, as well as the elaborated substantial activity and transparency factors, to the preferential regimes of members and associates. However, the elaborated substantial activity factor has so far only been applied to IP regimes. In respect of substantial activity the IP regimes reviewed were all considered inconsistent, either in whole or in part, with the nexus approach as described in this report. This reflects the fact that, unlike other aspects of the work on harmful tax practices, the details of this approach were only finalised during the BEPS Project while the regimes had been designed at an earlier point in time. Countries with such regimes will now proceed with a review of possible amendments of the relevant features of their regimes. The FHTP's work on reviewing preferential regimes will continue, recognising also that regimes that were assessed before the substantial activity requirement was elaborated may need to be reassessed.

Next steps

The elements of a strategy to engage with countries other than OECD Members and BEPS Associates in order to achieve a level playing field and avoid the risk that the work on harmful tax practices could displace regimes to third countries is outlined in the Report, together with the status of discussions on the revisions or additions to the existing framework. These aspects of the work will be taken forward in the context of the wider objective of designing a more inclusive framework to support and monitor the implementation of the BEPS measures.

An ongoing monitoring and review mechanism covering preferential regimes, including IP regimes, and the transparency framework has been agreed and will now be put in place.

Chapter 1

Introduction and background

1. At its June 2013 meeting, the Committee on Fiscal Affairs (CFA) of the Organisation for Economic Co-operation and Development (OECD) approved the *Action Plan on Base Erosion and Profit Shifting* (BEPS Action Plan, OECD, 2013a) which was subsequently endorsed by the G20 Finance Ministers at their July 2013 meeting and by the G20 Leaders at their September 2013 meeting. In response to the call in the report *Addressing Base Erosion and Profit Shifting* (BEPS Report, OECD, 2013b) to develop "solutions to counter harmful regimes more effectively, taking into account factors such as transparency and substance",[1] Action 5 of the BEPS Action Plan commits the Forum on Harmful Tax Practices (FHTP) to the following:[2]

> *Revamp the work on harmful tax practices with a priority on improving transparency, including compulsory spontaneous exchange on rulings related to preferential regimes, and on requiring substantial activity for any preferential regime. It will take a holistic approach to evaluate preferential tax regimes in the BEPS context. It will engage with non-OECD members on the basis of the existing framework and consider revisions or additions to the existing framework.* (OECD, 2013a)

2. As is clear from Action 5, work in this area is not new. In 1998, the OECD published the report *Harmful Tax Competition: An Emerging Global Issue* (1998 Report, OECD, 1998). This report laid the foundations for the OECD's work in the area of harmful tax practices and created the FHTP to take forward this work. It was published in response to a request by Ministers to develop measures to counter harmful tax practices with respect to geographically mobile activities, such as financial and other service activities, including the provision of intangibles. The nature of those types of activities makes it very easy to shift them from one country to another. Globalisation and technological innovation have further enhanced that mobility. The goal of the OECD's work in the area of harmful tax practices is to secure the integrity of tax systems by addressing the issues raised by regimes that apply to mobile activities and that unfairly erode the tax bases of other countries, potentially distorting the location of capital and services. Such practices can also cause undesired shifts of part of the tax burden to less mobile tax bases, such as labour, property, and consumption, and increase administrative costs and compliance burdens on tax authorities and taxpayers.

3. The work on harmful tax practices is not intended to promote the harmonisation of income taxes or tax structures generally within or outside the OECD, nor is it about dictating to any country what should be the appropriate level of tax rates. Rather, the work is about reducing the distortionary influence of taxation on the location of mobile financial and service activities, thereby encouraging an environment in which free and fair tax competition can take place. This is essential in moving towards a "level playing

field" and a continued expansion of global economic growth. Countries have long recognised that a "race to the bottom" would ultimately drive applicable tax rates on certain sources of income to zero for all countries, whether or not this is the tax policy a country wishes to pursue, and combating harmful tax practices is an interest common to OECD and non-OECD countries alike. There are obvious limitations to the effectiveness of unilateral actions against such practices. By agreeing a set of common criteria and promoting a co-operative framework, the work not only supports the effective fiscal sovereignty of countries over the design of their tax systems but it also enhances the ability of countries to react against the harmful tax practices of others.

4. More than 15 years have passed since the publication of the 1998 Report but the underlying policy concerns expressed in the 1998 Report have not lost their relevance. In certain areas, current concerns may be less about traditional ring-fencing but instead relate to across the board corporate tax rate reductions on particular types of income (such as income from financial activities or from the provision of intangibles). The fact that preferential regimes continue to be a pressure area is highlighted by their inclusion in the BEPS Report[3] and Action 5 of the BEPS Action Plan.[4]

5. Under Action 5, the FHTP is to deliver the following three outputs:

- First, finalisation of the review of member and associate country preferential regimes
- Second, a strategy to expand participation to third countries
- Third, consideration of revisions or additions to the existing framework.

6. In September 2014 the OECD released an initial progress report of the FHTP's progress on these outputs, *Countering Harmful Tax Practices More Effectively, Taking into Account Transparency and Substance* (2014 Progress Report, OECD, 2014). This report is the final report on Action 5, and it incorporates and supersedes the 2014 Progress Report.

Notes

1. See Chapter 5 of the BEPS Report – Addressing concerns related to base erosion and profit shifting, p. 53.
2. See Action 5 of the BEPS Action Plan – Counter harmful tax practices more effectively, taking into account transparency and substance, p. 18.
3. See Chapter 5 of the BEPS Report – Addressing concerns related to base erosion and profit shifting, p. 48.
4. See Action 5 of the BEPS Action Plan – Counter harmful tax practices more effectively, taking into account transparency and substance, p. 17.

Bibliography

OECD (2014), *Countering Harmful Tax Practices More Effectively, Taking into Account Transparency and Substance*, OECD Publishing, Paris, http://dx.doi.org/10.1787/9789264218970-en.

OECD (2013a), *Action Plan on Base Erosion and Profit Shifting*, OECD Publishing, Paris, http://dx.doi.org/10.1787/9789264202719-en.

OECD (2013b), *Addressing Base Erosion and Profit Shifting*, OECD Publishing, Paris, http://dx.doi.org/10.1787/9789264192744-en.

OECD (1998), *Harmful Tax Competition: An Emerging Global Issue*, OECD Publishing, Paris, http://dx.doi.org/10.1787/9789264162945-en.

Chapter 2

Overview of the OECD's work on harmful tax practices

7. The 1998 Report (OECD, 1998) divided the work on harmful tax practices into three areas: (i) preferential regimes in OECD countries, (ii) tax havens and (iii) non-OECD economies. The 1998 Report set out four key factors and eight other factors to determine whether a preferential regime is potentially harmful[1] and four key factors used to define "tax havens".[2] The 1998 Report was followed by four progress reports:

a) The first report, issued in June (2000 Report, OECD, 2001), outlined the progress made and, among other things, identified 47 potentially harmful regimes within OECD countries as well as 35 jurisdictions found to have met the tax haven criteria (in addition to the six jurisdictions meeting the criteria that had made advance commitments to eliminate harmful tax practices).

b) A second progress report was released in 2001 (OECD, 2002a). It made several important modifications to the tax haven aspect of the work. Most importantly, it provided that in determining which jurisdictions would be considered as uncooperative tax havens, commitments would be sought only with respect to the principles of effective exchange of information and transparency.

c) Between 2000 and 2004, generic guidance, or "application", notes were developed to assist member countries in reviewing existing or future preferential regimes and in assessing whether any of the factors in the 1998 Report are present. Application notes were developed on transparency and exchange of information, ring-fencing, transfer pricing, rulings, holding companies, fund management, and shipping. The separate application notes were combined into a single Consolidated Application Note (CAN, OECD, 2004a).

d) In early 2004, the OECD issued another report (2004 Report, OECD, 2004b) which focused mainly on the progress made with respect to eliminating harmful aspects of preferential regimes in OECD countries. In addition to the 47 regimes identified in 2000, the report included determinations on holding companies and similar preferential regimes. A number of regimes that had been introduced since the initial identification of potentially harmful regimes in 2000 were also considered but none of these regimes were found to be harmful within the meaning of the 1998 Report.

e) Finally, a report on OECD country preferential regimes was issued in September 2006 (OECD, 2006). Of the 47 regimes initially identified as potentially harmful in the 2000 Report, 46 were abolished, amended or found not to be harmful following further analysis. Only one preferential regime was found to be actually harmful and legislation was subsequently enacted by the relevant country to abolish this regime.

8. Over time, the work relating to the tax haven aspects was increasingly carried out through the Global Forum on Taxation (Global Forum), which was created in the early 2000s to engage in a dialogue with non-OECD countries on tax issues. The jurisdictions that had committed to the principles of effective exchange of information on request and transparency were invited to participate in the Global Forum, along with OECD countries, to further articulate the principles of effective exchange of information on request and transparency and to ensure their implementation. In 2002, the Global Forum developed the *Agreement on Exchange of Information in Tax Matters* (OECD, 2002b), and in 2005 it agreed standards on transparency relating to availability and reliability of information. Since 2006, the Global Forum has published annual assessments of progress in implementing the standards.[3]

9. In September 2009, the Global Forum was renamed the Global Forum on Transparency and Exchange of Information for Tax Purposes, and was restructured to expand its membership and its mandate and to improve its governance.[4] Subsequently, the CFA decided to restructure the bodies responsible for Exchange of Information (EOI) by creating Working Party No. 10 on Exchange of Information and Tax Compliance to take over the responsibilities of Working Party No. 8 on Tax Avoidance and Evasion, as well as the EOI matters previously addressed by the FHTP.[5] Going forward, the work of the FHTP has therefore focused on preferential tax regimes and on defensive measures in respect of such regimes (other than any such measures related to a lack of EOI or transparency).

Notes

1. Those factors and the process for determining whether a regime is a harmful preferential regime under the framework of the 1998 Report are described below under Chapter 3, Section II.

2. The four key factors to define a "tax haven" were: (i) no or nominal tax on the relevant income; (ii) lack of effective exchange of information; (iii) lack of transparency; (iv) no substantial activities. No or nominal tax is not sufficient in itself to classify a jurisdiction as a tax haven.

3. The relevant reports can be accessed on the following webpage: www.oecd.org/tax/transparency/keypublications.htm.

4. Information on the Global Forum on Transparency and Exchange of Information for Tax Purposes and its work is available at: www.oecd.org/tax/transparency.

5. Defensive measures related to a lack of exchange of information on request or transparency fall within the mandate of Working Party No. 10 on Exchange of Information and Tax Compliance. Action 5, however, requests the FHTP to "[r]evamp the work on harmful tax practices with a priority on improving transparency", and under this mandate, the FHTP has considered the ruling regimes in member and associate countries and developed a general best practices framework for the design and operation of ruling regimes, as described below under Chapter 5.

Bibliography

OECD (2006), *The OECD's Project on Harmful Tax Practices: 2006 Update on Progress in Member Countries*, OECD, www.oecd.org/ctp/harmful/37446434.pdf.

OECD (2004a), *Consolidated Application Note: Guidance in Applying the 1998 Report to Preferential Tax Regimes*, OECD, www.oecd.org/ctp/harmful/30901132.pdf.

OECD (2004b), *Harmful Tax Practices: The 2004 Progress Report*, OECD, www.oecd.org/ctp/harmful/30901115.pdf.

OECD (2002a), *The OECD's Project on Harmful Tax Practices: The 2001 Progress Report*, OECD Publishing, Paris, http://dx.doi.org/10.1787/9789264033993-en.

OECD (2002b), *Agreement on Exchange of Information in Tax Matters*, OECD Publishing, Paris, http://dx.doi.org/10.1787/9789264034853-en.

OECD (2001), *Towards Global Tax Co-operation: Progress in Identifying and Eliminating Harmful Tax Practices*, OECD Publishing, Paris, http://dx.doi.org/10.1787/9789264184541-en.

OECD (1998), *Harmful Tax Competition: An Emerging Global Issue*, OECD Publishing, Paris, http://dx.doi.org/10.1787/9789264162945-en.

Bibliography

Chapter 3

Framework under the 1998 Report for determining whether a regime is a harmful preferential regime

10. This Chapter describes the framework under the 1998 Report (OECD, 1998) for determining whether a regime is a harmful preferential regime. This involves three stages:

a) Consideration of whether a regime is within the scope of work of the FHTP and whether it is preferential;

b) Consideration of the four key factors and eight other factors set out in the 1998 Report to determine whether a preferential regime is potentially harmful;

c) Consideration of the economic effects of a regime to determine whether a potentially harmful regime is actually harmful.

A. Consideration of whether a regime is within the scope of work of the FHTP and whether it is preferential

Scope of work of the FHTP

11. To be within the scope of the 1998 Report, the regime must, firstly, apply to income from geographically mobile activities, such as financial and other service activities, including the provision of intangibles. Preferential regimes designed to attract investment in plant, building and equipment are outside the scope of the 1998 Report.[1]

12. Secondly, the regime must relate to the taxation of the relevant income from geographically mobile activities. Hence, the work is mainly concerned with business taxation. Consumption taxes are explicitly excluded.[2] Business taxes may be levied at national, federal or central government level ("national taxes") and/or at sub-national, sub-federal or decentralised level ("sub-national taxes"). Sub-national taxes include taxes levied at state, regional, provincial or local level. In the course of the current review, the question arose as to whether regimes offering tax benefits at sub-national level alone ("sub-national regimes") are within the scope of the FHTP's work. This is discussed in Chapter 6.

Preferential tax treatment

13. In order for a regime to be considered preferential, it must offer some form of tax preference in comparison with the general principles of taxation in the relevant country. A preference offered by a regime may take a wide range of forms, including a reduction in the tax rate or tax base or preferential terms for the payment or repayment of taxes. Even a small amount of preference is sufficient for the regime to be considered preferential. The key point is that the regime must be preferential *in comparison with the general principles of taxation in the relevant country*, and not in comparison with

principles applied in other countries. For example, where the rate of corporate tax applied to all income in a particular country is 10%, the taxation of income from mobile activities at 10% is not preferential, even though it may be lower than the rate applied in other countries.

B. Consideration of the four key factors and eight other factors set out in the 1998 Report to determine whether a preferential regime is potentially harmful

14. Four key factors and eight other factors are used to determine whether a preferential regime within the scope of the FHTP's work is potentially harmful.[3] A reference to substantial activity is already included in the eight other factors so this is not a new concept. The eight other factors generally help to spell out, in more detail, some of the key principles and assumptions that should be considered in applying the key factors themselves.

15. The four key factors are:

a) The regime imposes no or low effective tax rates on income from geographically mobile financial and other service activities.

b) The regime is ring-fenced from the domestic economy.

c) The regime lacks transparency (for example, the details of the regime or its application are not apparent, or there is inadequate regulatory supervision or financial disclosure).

d) There is no effective exchange of information with respect to the regime.[4]

16. The eight other factors are:

a) An artificial definition of the tax base.

b) Failure to adhere to international transfer pricing principles.

c) Foreign source income exempt from residence country taxation.

d) Negotiable tax rate or tax base.

e) Existence of secrecy provisions.

f) Access to a wide network of tax treaties.

g) The regime is promoted as a tax minimisation vehicle.

h) The regime encourages operations or arrangements that are purely tax-driven and involve no substantial activities.

17. In order for a regime to be considered potentially harmful, the first key factor, "no or low effective tax rate", must apply. This is a gateway criterion. Where a regime offers tax benefits at both national and sub-national level, the question of whether the regime meets the low or no effective tax rate factor is, generally, determined based on the combined effective tax rate for both the national and sub-national levels. The reduction in national taxes alone may, in some cases, be considered sufficient to determine that entities benefiting from the regime are subject to a low or no effective tax rate. The application of the no or low effective tax rate factor to regimes offering tax benefits at sub-national level alone is discussed in Chapter 6.

18. Where a regime meets the no or low effective tax rate factor, an evaluation of whether that regime is potentially harmful should be based on an overall assessment of each of the other three "key factors" and, where relevant, the eight "other factors". Where low or zero effective taxation and one or more of the remaining factors apply, a regime will be characterised as potentially harmful.

C. Consideration of the economic effects of a regime to determine whether a potentially harmful regime is actually harmful

19. A regime that has been identified as being potentially harmful based on the above factor analysis may be considered not to be actually harmful if it does not appear to have created harmful economic effects.

20. The following three questions can be helpful in making this assessment:

- Does the tax regime shift activity from one country to the country providing the preferential tax regime, rather than generate significant new activity?
- Is the presence and level of activities in the host country commensurate with the amount of investment or income?
- Is the preferential regime the primary motivation for the location of an activity?[5]

21. Following consideration of its economic effects, a regime that has created harmful effects will be categorised as a harmful preferential regime.

22. Where a preferential regime has been found to be actually harmful, the relevant country is given the opportunity to abolish the regime or remove the features that create the harmful effect. Other countries may take defensive measures to counter the effects of the harmful regime, while at the same time continuing to encourage the country applying the regime to modify or remove it.[6] It is recognised that countries' defensive measures may also apply in situations which do not involve harmful preferential regimes as defined in the 1998 Report. The 1998 Report does not affect countries' right to use such measures in such situations.[7]

Notes

1. See paragraph 6 of 1998 Report, p. 8.
2. See paragraph 7 of 1998 Report, p. 8.
3. See paragraphs 59-79 of 1998 Report, pp. 25-34.
4. Note that in assessing transparency and effective exchange of information factors, the FHTP looks specifically at how a particular regime measures up against those factors. It does not attempt to revisit the work of the Global Forum, which has a broader and more general focus on transparency and effective exchange of information more generally. However, to the extent that the work of the Global Forum highlights certain issues with respect to a particular regime, these are taken into account in the FHTP's evaluations.
5. See paragraphs 80-84 of 1998 Report for more details on each of those questions, pp. 34-35.
6. See paragraph 96 of 1998 Report, p. 40.
7. See paragraph 98 of 1998 Report which states this principle with respect to controlled foreign company (CFC) rules specifically, p. 41.

Bibliography

OECD (1998), *Harmful Tax Competition: An Emerging Global Issue*, OECD Publishing, Paris, http://dx.doi.org/10.1787/9789264162945-en.

Chapter 4

Revamp of the work on harmful tax practices: Substantial activity requirement

23. To counter harmful regimes more effectively, Action 5 of the BEPS Action Plan (OECD, 2013) requires the FHTP to revamp the work on harmful tax practices, with a priority and renewed focus on requiring substantial activity for any preferential regime and on improving transparency, including compulsory spontaneous exchange on rulings related to preferential regimes. This Chapter describes the work carried out by the FHTP in the first of these two priority areas. The discussion on substantial activity in this Chapter builds on and incorporates the discussion in the 2014 Progress Report (OECD, 2014) to ensure that all discussions of the nexus approach are combined in one report. This Chapter is therefore fully self-standing and contains all the guidance on the nexus approach and its application in the context of regimes which provide a preferential tax treatment for certain income arising from qualifying intellectual property ("IP regimes").

I. Introduction

24. Action 5 specifically requires substantial activity for any preferential regime. Seen in the wider context of the work on BEPS, this requirement contributes to the second pillar of the BEPS Project, which is to align taxation with substance by ensuring that taxable profits can no longer be artificially shifted away from the countries where value is created. The framework set out in the 1998 Report (OECD, 1998) already contains a substantial activity requirement. This requirement is grounded in particular in the twelfth factor (i.e. the eighth other factor) set out in the 1998 Report. This factor looks at whether a regime "encourages purely tax-driven operations or arrangements" and states that "many harmful preferential tax regimes are designed in a way that allows taxpayers to derive benefits from the regime while engaging in operations that are purely tax-driven and involve no substantial activities". The 1998 Report contains limited guidance on how to apply this factor.

25. The substantial activity factor has been elevated in importance under Action 5, which mandates that this factor be elaborated in the context of BEPS. This factor will then be considered along with the four key factors when determining whether a preferential regime within the scope of the FHTP's work is potentially harmful. The FHTP considered various approaches to applying the substantial activity factor in the context of IP regimes. There is a clear link between this work and statements in the BEPS Action Plan that current concerns in the area of harmful tax practices may be less about traditional ring-fencing and instead relate to corporate tax rate reductions on particular types of income, such as income from the provision of intangibles.[1] All IP regimes in OECD countries and associate countries have been reviewed at the same time as part of the current review and none of these regimes had been reviewed as part of the earlier

work. The elaborated substantial activity requirement can therefore be applied without needing to re-assess IP regimes previously reviewed. Under Action 5, the substantial activity requirement applies to all preferential regimes within scope, including non-IP regimes, and the FHTP has also considered this aspect.

II. Substantial activity requirement in the context of IP regimes

26. Regimes that provide for a tax preference on income relating to IP raise the base-eroding concerns that are the focus of the FHTP's work. At the same time, it is recognised that IP-intensive industries are a key driver of growth and employment and that countries are free to provide tax incentives for research and development (R&D) activities, provided that they are granted according to the principles agreed by the FHTP. The approach adopted by the FHTP to requiring substantial activity is therefore not intended to recommend any particular IP regime, but it is instead designed to describe the outer limits of an IP regime that grants benefits to R&D but does not have harmful effects on other countries. The FHTP makes no recommendation on the introduction of IP regimes and jurisdictions remain free to decide whether or not to implement an IP regime. IP regimes that provide benefits to a narrower set of income, IP assets, expenditures, or taxpayers than that outlined below would also be consistent with the FHTP's approach.

27. The FHTP considered three different approaches to requiring substantial activities in an IP regime. The first approach was a value creation approach that required taxpayers to undertake a set number of significant development activities. This approach did not have any support over the other two. The second approach was a transfer pricing approach that would allow a regime to provide benefits to all the income generated by the IP if the taxpayer had located a set level of important functions in the jurisdiction providing the regime, if the taxpayer is the legal owner of the assets giving rise to the tax benefits and uses the assets giving rise to the tax benefits, and if the taxpayer bears the economic risks of the assets giving rise to the tax benefits. A few countries supported the transfer pricing approach, but many countries raised a number of concerns with the transfer pricing approach, which is why the work of the FHTP did not focus further on this approach. The third approach was the nexus approach, which has been agreed by the FHTP and endorsed by the G20.[2]

28. This approach looks to whether an IP regime makes its benefits conditional on the extent of R&D activities of taxpayers receiving benefits. The approach seeks to build on the basic principle underlying R&D credits and similar "front-end" tax regimes that apply to expenditures incurred in the creation of IP. Under these front-end regimes, the expenditures and benefits are directly linked because the expenditures are used to calculate the tax benefit. The nexus approach extends this principle to apply to "back-end" tax regimes that apply to the income earned after the creation and exploitation of the IP. Thus, rather than limiting jurisdictions to IP regimes that only provide benefits directly to the expenditures incurred to create the IP, the nexus approach also permits jurisdictions to provide benefits to the income arising out of that IP, so long as there is a direct nexus between the income receiving benefits and the expenditures contributing to that income. This focus on expenditures aligns with the underlying purpose of IP regimes by ensuring that the regimes that are intended to encourage R&D activity only provide benefits to taxpayers that in fact engage in such activity.

29. Expenditures therefore act as a proxy for substantial activities. It is not the *amount* of expenditures that acts as a direct proxy for the amount of activities. It is instead the *proportion* of expenditures directly related to development activities that demonstrates

real value added by the taxpayer and acts as a proxy for how much substantial activity the taxpayer undertook. The nexus approach applies a proportionate analysis to income, under which the proportion of income that may benefit from an IP regime is the same proportion as that between qualifying expenditures and overall expenditures. In other words, the nexus approach allows a regime to provide for a preferential rate on IP-related income to the extent it was generated by qualifying expenditures. The purpose of the nexus approach is to grant benefits only to income that arises from IP where the actual R&D activity was undertaken by the taxpayer itself. This goal is achieved by defining "qualifying expenditures" in such a way that they effectively prevent mere capital contribution or expenditures for substantial R&D activity by parties other than the taxpayer from qualifying the subsequent income for benefits under an IP regime.

30. If a company only had one IP asset and had itself incurred all of the expenditures to develop that asset, the nexus approach would simply allow all of the income from that IP asset to qualify for benefits. Once a company's business model becomes more complicated, however, the nexus approach also by necessity becomes more complicated, because the approach must determine a nexus between multiple strands of income and expenditure, only some of which may be qualifying expenditures. In order to address this complexity, the nexus approach apportions income according to a ratio of expenditures. The nexus approach determines what income may receive tax benefits by applying the following calculation:

$$\frac{\textbf{Qualifying expenditures incurred to develop IP asset}}{\textbf{Overall expenditures incurred to develop IP asset}} \times \textbf{Overall income from IP asset} = \textbf{Income receiving tax benefits}$$

31. The ratio in this calculation ("the nexus ratio") only includes qualifying and overall expenditures incurred by the entity. It therefore does not consider all expenditures ever incurred in the development of the IP asset. As will be explained in the following discussions of qualifying expenditures and overall expenditures, a qualifying taxpayer that did not acquire the IP asset or outsource the development of that IP asset to a related party would therefore have a ratio of 100%, which would apply to the entity's overall income from the IP asset. This in turn means that the nexus approach was not designed to disadvantage arrangements where different entities are engaged in activities contributing to the development of IP assets.[3]

32. Where the amount of income receiving benefits under an IP regime does not exceed the amount determined by the nexus approach, the regime has met the substantial activity requirement. The remainder of this section provides further guidance on the application of the nexus approach and the above calculation.

A. Qualifying taxpayers

33. Qualifying taxpayers would include resident companies, domestic permanent establishments (PEs) of foreign companies, and foreign PEs of resident companies that are subject to tax in the jurisdiction providing benefits. The expenditures incurred by a PE cannot qualify income earned by the head office as qualifying income if the PE is not operating at the time that income is earned.[4]

B. IP assets

34. Under the nexus approach as contemplated, the only IP assets that could qualify for tax benefits under an IP regime are patents and other IP assets that are functionally equivalent to patents if those IP assets are both legally protected[5] and subject to similar approval and registration processes, where such processes are relevant. IP assets that are functionally equivalent to patents are (i) patents defined broadly, (ii) copyrighted software, and (iii) in certain circumstances set out below, other IP assets that are non-obvious, useful, and novel.

35. For purposes of the first category of functionally equivalent assets, patents that qualify under the nexus approach are not just patents in a narrow sense of the word but also utility models, IP assets that grant protection to plants and genetic material, orphan drug designations, and extensions of patent protection. Utility models, irrespective of their designation under domestic law (e.g. "petty patents", "innovation patents", "short term patents"), are generally provided to incremental inventions, have a less rigorous patent process, and provide patent protection for a shorter time period. IP assets that grant protection to plants and genetic material would include plant breeders' rights, which grant exclusive control over new varieties of plants. Orphan drug designations are provided by government agencies for certain pharmaceuticals that are developed to treat rare diseases or diseases that are not likely to lead to significant profits and these designations grant exclusive rights to the innovations. Extensions of patent protection such as supplementary protection certificates extend the exclusive right of certain patents for pharmaceuticals and plant protection products, and they recognise that the time needed to research and develop these IP assets is generally longer than the time needed to research and develop other IP assets and therefore justifies that the protected life of the asset should extend past the duration of the patent. Therefore, IP assets in the first category cover patents in the broad sense, including the extension of patent protection.

36. Copyrighted software[6] shares the fundamental characteristics of patents, since it is novel, non-obvious, and useful. It arises from the type of innovation and R&D that IP regimes are typically designed to encourage, and taxpayers in the software industry are unlikely to outsource the development of their core software to unrelated parties. Copyrighted software therefore is the second category of functionally equivalent assets, but other copyrighted assets are not included in the definition of functionally equivalent IP assets because they do not arise out of the same type of R&D activities as software.

37. Qualifying IP assets can also include IP assets that do not fall into either of the first two categories but that share features of patents (i.e. are non-obvious, useful, and novel), are substantially similar to the IP assets in the first two categories, and are certified as such in a transparent certification process by a competent government agency that is independent from the tax administration. Such a certification process must also provide for full transparency on the types of assets covered. The only taxpayers that may qualify for such benefits are those that have no more than EUR 50 million (or a near equivalent amount in domestic currency) in global group-wide turnover and that do not themselves earn more than EUR 7.5 million per year (or a near equivalent amount in domestic currency) in gross revenues from all IP assets, using a five-year average for both calculations.[7] Jurisdictions that provide benefits to income from the third category of IP assets should notify the FHTP that they provide such benefits and should provide information on the applicable legal and administrative framework. They should provide information to the FHTP on the number of each type of IP asset included in the third category, the number of taxpayers benefiting from the third category, and the aggregate

amount of IP income arising from the third category of IP assets that qualifies for the IP regime. Jurisdictions would also need to spontaneously exchange information on taxpayers benefiting from the third category of IP assets, using the framework set out in Chapter 5.[8] The FHTP will proceed to a review of the third category of IP assets no later than 2020.

38. The nexus approach focuses on establishing a nexus between expenditures, these IP assets, and income. Under the nexus approach, marketing-related IP assets such as trademarks can never qualify for tax benefits under an IP regime.[9]

C. *Qualifying expenditures*

39. Qualifying expenditures must have been incurred by a qualifying taxpayer, and they must be directly connected to the IP asset. Jurisdictions will provide their own definitions of qualifying expenditures, and such definitions must ensure that qualifying expenditures only include expenditures that are incurred for the purpose of actual R&D activities. They would include the types of expenditures that currently qualify for R&D credits under the tax laws of multiple jurisdictions.[10] They would not include interest payments, building costs, acquisition costs, or any costs that could not be directly linked to a specific IP asset.[11] However, where expenditures for general and speculative R&D cannot be included in the qualifying expenditures of a specific IP asset to which they have a direct link, they could be divided pro rata across IP assets or products. Qualifying expenditures will be included in the nexus calculation at the time they are incurred, regardless of their treatment for accounting or other tax purposes. In other words, expenditures that are not fully deductible in the year in which they were incurred because they are capitalised will still be included in full in the nexus ratio starting in the year in which they were incurred. This timing rule only applies for purposes of the nexus ratio, and it is not intended to change any timing rules in jurisdictions' domestic tax rules.

40. When calculating qualifying expenditures, jurisdictions may permit taxpayers to apply a 30% "up-lift" to expenditures that are included in qualifying expenditures. This up-lift may increase qualifying expenditures but only to the extent that the taxpayer has non-qualifying expenditures. In other words, the increased amount of qualifying expenditures may not exceed the taxpayer's overall expenditures. This is illustrated in the examples below:

- Example A: The taxpayer itself incurred qualifying expenditures of 100, it incurred acquisition costs of 10, and it paid 40 for the R&D expenditures of a related party. The initial amount of qualifying expenditures is therefore 100, and the maximum up-lift will be 30 (i.e. 100 x 30%). The taxpayer can only increase its qualifying expenditures to 130 if its overall expenditures are equal to or greater than 130. Overall expenditures in this example are equal to 150, so the up-lift can increase qualifying expenditures to 130. IP income will therefore be multiplied by 130/150 (or 86.7%).

- Example B: The taxpayer itself incurred qualifying expenditures of 100, it incurred acquisition costs of 5, and it paid 20 for the R&D expenditures of a related party. The maximum up-lift would again increase qualifying expenditures to 130, but the taxpayer in this example only has 125 of overall expenditures. The up-lift can therefore only increase qualifying expenditures to 125, and IP income will therefore be multiplied by 125/125 (or 100%).

41. The purpose of the up-lift is to ensure that the nexus approach does not penalise taxpayers excessively for acquiring IP or outsourcing R&D activities to related parties. The up-lift still ensures that taxpayers only receive benefits if they themselves undertook R&D activities, but it acknowledges that taxpayers that acquired IP or outsourced a portion of the R&D to a related party may themselves still be responsible for much of the value creation that contributed to IP income.

D. Overall expenditures

42. Overall expenditures should be defined in such a way that, if the qualifying taxpayer incurred all relevant expenditures itself, the ratio would allow 100% of the income from the IP asset to benefit from the preferential regime. This means that overall expenditures must be the sum of all expenditures that would count as qualifying expenditures if they were undertaken by the taxpayer itself. This in turn means that any expenditures that would not be included in qualifying expenditures even if incurred by the taxpayer itself (e.g. interest payments, building costs, and other costs that do not represent actual R&D activities) cannot be included in overall expenditures and hence do not affect the amount of income that may benefit from an IP regime. IP acquisition costs are an exception, since they are included in overall expenditures and not in qualifying expenditures. Their exclusion is consistent with the principle of what is included in overall expenditures, however, because they are a proxy for expenditures incurred by a non-qualifying taxpayer. Overall expenditures therefore include all qualifying expenditures, acquisition costs, and expenditures for outsourcing that do not count as qualifying expenditures.

43. The nexus approach therefore does not include all expenditures ever incurred in the development of an IP asset in overall expenditures. Instead, it only adds two things to qualifying expenditures: expenditures for related-party outsourcing and acquisition costs.[12] The nexus ratio can therefore be written as:

$$\frac{a+b}{a+b+c+d}$$

44. In this version of the nexus ratio, *a* represents R&D expenditures incurred by the taxpayer itself, *b* represents expenditures for unrelated-party outsourcing, *c* represents acquisition costs, and *d* represents expenditures for related-party outsourcing. This means that the only way that the ratio can be decreased from 100% is if the taxpayer outsourced the R&D to related parties or acquired the R&D. Expenditures for unsuccessful R&D will typically not be included in the nexus ratio, which is consistent with the purposes of IP regimes that grant benefits to income, since unsuccessful R&D by definition does not generate any income. If, however, R&D expenditures were incurred by the taxpayer or outsourced to unrelated parties in connection with a larger R&D project that produced an income-generating IP asset, then an IP regime may also include all such R&D expenditures in qualifying expenditures and not just those R&D expenditures that, with the benefit of hindsight, directly contributed to IP income. These expenditures could be treated the same as general or speculative R&D and either divided pro rata across IP assets or included in qualifying expenditures if a direct link between the IP asset and the expenditures could be established. As in the context of qualifying expenditures, overall expenditures will be included in the nexus calculation at the time they are incurred, regardless of their treatment for accounting or other tax purposes. This timing rule only applies for purposes of the nexus ratio, and it is not intended to change any timing rules in

jurisdictions' tax rules insofar as they apply for other purposes, including the computation of overall income derived from the IP asset.[13]

45. Often, overall expenditures will be incurred prior to the production of income that could qualify for benefits under the IP regime. The nexus approach is an additive approach, and the calculation requires both that "qualifying expenditures" include all qualifying expenditures incurred by the taxpayer over the life of the IP asset and that "overall expenditures" include all overall expenditures incurred over the life of the IP asset. These numbers will therefore increase every time a taxpayer incurs expenditure that would qualify for either category. The proportion of the cumulative numbers will then determine the percentage to be applied to overall income earned each year.

E. Overall income

46. Jurisdictions will define "overall income" consistent with their domestic laws on income definition after the application of transfer pricing rules. The definition that they choose should comply with the following principles:

Income benefiting from the regime should be proportionate

47. Overall income should be defined in such a way that the income that benefits from the regime is not disproportionately high given the percentage of qualifying expenditures undertaken by qualifying taxpayers. This means that overall income should not be defined as the gross income from the IP asset, since such a definition could allow 100% of the net income of qualifying taxpayers to benefit even when those taxpayers had not incurred 100% of qualifying expenditures. Overall income should instead be calculated by subtracting IP expenditures allocable to IP income and incurred in the year from gross IP income earned in the year.[14]

Overall income should be limited to IP income

48. Overall income should only include income that is derived from the IP asset. This may include royalties, capital gains and other income from the sale of an IP asset, and embedded IP income from the sale of products and the use of processes directly related to the IP asset. Jurisdictions that choose to grant benefits to embedded IP income must implement a consistent and coherent method for separating income unrelated to IP (e.g. marketing and manufacturing returns) from the income arising from IP. One method that would achieve this outcome could, for example, be based on transfer pricing principles.[15]

F. Outsourcing

49. The nexus approach is intended to ensure that, in order for a significant proportion of IP income to qualify for benefits, a significant proportion of the actual R&D activities must have been undertaken by the qualifying taxpayer itself. The nexus approach would allow all qualifying expenditures for activities undertaken by unrelated parties (whether or not they were within the jurisdiction) to qualify, while all expenditures for activities undertaken by related parties – again, whether or not they were within the jurisdiction – would not count as qualifying expenditures.[16]

50. As a matter of business practice, unlimited outsourcing to unrelated parties should not provide many opportunities for taxpayers to receive benefits without themselves engaging in substantial activities because, while a company may outsource the full spectrum of R&D activities to a related party, the same is typically not true of an

unrelated party. Since the vast majority of the value of an IP asset rests in both the R&D undertaken to create it and the information necessary to undertake such R&D, it is unlikely that a company will outsource the fundamental value-creating activities to an unrelated party, regardless of where that unrelated party is located.[17] Allowing only expenditures incurred by unrelated parties to be treated as qualifying expenditures thus achieves the goal of the nexus approach to only grant tax benefits to income arising from the substantive R&D activities in which the taxpayer itself engaged that contributed to the income. Jurisdictions could narrow the definition of unrelated parties to include only universities, hospitals, R&D centres and non-profit entities that were unrelated to the qualifying taxpayer. Where a payment is made through a related party to an unrelated party without any margin, the payment will be included in qualifying expenditures.

51. Jurisdictions could also only permit unrelated outsourcing up to a certain percentage or proportion (while still excluding outsourcing to related parties from the definition of qualifying expenditures). As explained above, business realities typically mean that a company will not outsource more than an insubstantial amount of R&D activities to an unrelated party, so both a prohibition on outsourcing to any related parties and that same prohibition combined with a cap that prohibits outsourcing to unrelated parties beyond an insubstantial amount should have the equivalent effect of limiting qualifying expenditures to those expenditures incurred to support fundamental R&D activities by the taxpayer.

G. Treatment of acquired IP

52. The basic principle underlying the treatment of acquired IP by the nexus approach is that only the expenditures incurred for improving the IP asset after it was acquired should be treated as qualifying expenditures. In order to achieve this, the nexus approach would exclude acquisition costs from the definition of qualifying expenditures, as mentioned above, and only allow expenditures incurred after acquisition to be treated as qualifying expenditures. Acquisition costs would, however, be included in overall expenditures. Acquisition costs would include, among other expenditures, those that were incurred to obtain rights to research.[18] Acquisition costs (or, in the case of licensing, royalties or license fees) are a proxy for overall expenditures incurred prior to acquisition. Therefore, no expenditures incurred by any party prior to acquisition will be included in either qualifying expenditures or overall expenditures.[19] In the context of related party acquisitions, the arm's length price must be used to determine acquisition costs. Given that taxpayers may have an incentive to undervalue transfers between related parties into IP regimes, any related party acquisitions will require that taxpayers prepare documentation substantiating the arm's length price, including documentation on the overall expenditures that the related party transferor incurred. Acquisitions include any transfer of rights regardless of whether a payment was actually made.

H. Tracking of income and expenditures

53. Since the nexus approach depends on there being a nexus between expenditures and income, it requires jurisdictions wishing to introduce an IP regime to mandate that taxpayers that want to benefit from an IP regime must track expenditures, IP assets, and income to ensure that the income receiving benefits did in fact arise from the expenditures that qualified for those benefits. If a taxpayer has only one IP asset that it has fully self-developed and that provides all of its income, this tracking should be fairly simple, since all qualifying expenditures incurred by that company will determine the benefits to be granted to all the IP income earned by that company. Once a company has

more than one IP asset or engages in any degree of outsourcing or acquisition, however, tracking becomes essential. Tracking must also ensure that taxpayers have not manipulated the amount of overall expenditures to inflate the amount of income that may benefit from the regime. This means that taxpayers will need to be able to track the link between expenditures and income and provide evidence of this to their tax administrations. Not engaging in such tracking will not prevent taxpayers from earning IP income in a jurisdiction, but it will prevent them from benefiting from a preferential IP regime.

54. The main complexity associated with tracking arises from the fact that a preferential rate is applied to certain IP income, which is a function of the regime rather than the nexus approach, and existing IP regimes suggest that taxpayers are willing to comply with certain often complex requirements when an optional tax benefit is made conditional on such requirements. Because the nexus approach will standardise the requirements of IP regimes across jurisdictions, it may in the long term reduce the overall complexity that taxpayers that are benefiting from multiple IP regimes currently face.

55. The fundamental principle underlying the nexus approach is that income should only benefit from an IP regime to the extent that the taxpayer itself incurred the R&D expenditures that contributed to that IP. If the taxpayer instead acquired the IP or outsourced the R&D to a related party, the income that arose from acquired IP or outsourced R&D should not benefit from an IP regime. The nexus approach was designed to require a link between expenditures, IP assets, and IP income, and taxpayers must track to IP assets. However, where such tracking would be unrealistic and require arbitrary judgements, jurisdictions may also choose to allow the application of the nexus approach so that the nexus can be between expenditures, products arising from IP assets, and income. Such an approach would require taxpayers to include all qualifying expenditures linked to the development of all IP assets that contributed to the product in "qualifying expenditures" and to include all overall expenditures linked to the development of all IP assets that contributed to the product in "overall expenditures". This aggregate ratio would then be applied to overall income from the product that was directly linked to all the underlying IP assets. This approach would be consistent with the nexus approach in cases where multiple IP assets are incorporated into one product, but jurisdictions must ensure that this product-based approach requires accurate tracking of all qualifying and overall expenditure at the level of the product and that benefits expire at a fair and reasonable time (e.g. the average life of all IP assets).

56. The product-based approach acknowledges that R&D activities often may not be structured on an IP-asset-by-IP-asset basis and it may then be consistent with the nexus approach to track and trace to products. This is because R&D programmes and projects are generally focused on answering research questions or solving technical problems and it is only in a subsequent stage that there is any discussion of how to provide legal protection to the results of these projects. Often, the results of these projects will contribute to multiple IP assets. Where this is the case, forcing an allocation of R&D expenditures between or among different IP assets would require taxpayers to arbitrarily divide research projects along lines that did not exist at the time the projects were undertaken.

57. In using the product-based approach, jurisdictions should apply a purposive definition of products, under which the meaning of the product to which taxpayers track and trace cannot be so large as to include all the IP income or expenditures of a taxpayer engaged in a complex, IP-based business with multiple products and R&D projects or so

small as to require taxpayers to track and trace to a category that is entirely unrelated to innovation or business practices. For a company that produces multiple components for one type of product, which it then sells, for instance a truck, a product definition that permitted tracking and tracing to that truck, and allowing the taxpayer to allocate all its R&D expenditures and IP income to that one final product, would be too broad because the R&D and related IP assets underlying the different value driving components would not sufficiently overlap. For a company that for example produces hinges that are used in hundreds of industries, however, a product definition that required the taxpayer to track and trace to the specific type of hinge built for a specific type of truck would be too narrow as it would require the taxpayer to track and trace to a level of detail that did not relate to the actual innovation. In the first situation (whole truck), it would be more appropriate for the taxpayer to track and trace to the components. In the second situation (hinges), it would be more appropriate for the taxpayer to track to the groups of hinges that shared the same IP rather than to the products in which they are used. This also means that it would not be appropriate to require tracking by individual products if they had only minor variations but contained the same IP (e.g. medicines that are produced in different colours, dosages, or sizes). The definition of products can therefore include product families such as components for printer or computer producers, active compounds for the chemical industry, and therapeutic areas or narrower disease categories for the pharmaceutical industry.[20] In applying the product-based approach, jurisdictions should prevent taxpayers from tracking to a grouping that is so broad that it would include all the expenditures and income of an entity, but taxpayers may track to products (including product families) when these groupings include all the IP assets that arose from overlapping expenditures and contributed to overlapping streams of income.

58. A taxpayer that uses the product-based approach must provide documentation that the taxpayer was engaged in a sufficiently complex IP-related business that tracking to individual IP assets would be unrealistic and based on arbitrary judgements. To prevent manipulation, a taxpayer that tracks and traces to products (including product families) should be able to justify to a tax authority the appropriateness of this approach with reference to objective and verifiable information, for example the commonality of scientific, technological, or engineering challenges underlying the R&D expenditures and income, demonstrate its consistency with the organisation of R&D activities within the group and also apply the approach consistently over time.

59. Examples of tracking and tracing to IP assets or products arising from those IP assets are provided below. All examples assume that the taxpayers are resident in jurisdictions with IP regimes that are consistent with the nexus approach.

- Example A: Company A produces plastic lids for travel mugs. Company A has two patents, one of which applies to plastic lids for coffee mugs and one of which applies to plastic lids for tea mugs. The R&D responsible for the two patents was undertaken by different project teams of Company A employees. Company A is therefore an example of a taxpayer that would need to track and trace to IP assets. If it did not already do so, it would need to set up a tracking system that tracked income of coffee mugs and tea mugs separately.

- Example B: Company B produces hundreds of different types of printers, which are divided and managed along three different product families: large printer/copier combinations for office use, small personal printers for home use, and photo printers for professional-quality digital photos. Each product family contains several distinct product types. Company B engages in R&D to develop the printers, and this R&D contributes to 250 patents. 100 patents are relevant to all three product families, 50 are relevant only to the larger printer/copier combinations, 50 are relevant only to the small personal printers and 50 are relevant only to the photo printers. Company B's employees track their research time according to which product family they are working on or whether they are engaged in general or speculative R&D. Company B is therefore an example of a taxpayer that would need to track and trace to product families. If it did not already do so, it would need to set up a tracking system that tracked income of the three product families separately. The expenditures incurred to develop the 100 general patents would be divided across the product families, and the expenditures that are only relevant to individual product families would be allocated only to those product families. It would not be appropriate to track and trace to either IP assets or product types because Company B's R&D is shared across product families, so tracking and tracing to individual products could over-allocate expenditures to one individual printer or under-allocate expenditures to another individual printer.

- <u>Example C</u>: Company C is a pharmaceutical company which has thousands of patents and which produces hundreds of pharmaceutical products. Each patent contributes to multiple products, and each product uses multiple patents. Company C manages and tracks its R&D, including its employees' time, along the four different diseases that its products treat. The R&D undertaken for one disease generally does not overlap with the R&D undertaken for another disease, and the diseases are dissimilar enough that products for one disease are not used to treat another disease. Company C's expenditures cannot be tracked to individual products (since R&D expenditures would have to be divided across multiple products which could only be done on an arbitrary basis). Company C's income cannot be tracked to individual patents (because income for one product would have to be divided across multiple patents, requiring arbitrary allocations). Company C would therefore need to track and trace to the diseases that Company C's products are designed to treat. If it does not already do so, it would need to set up a tracking system that tracked IP income from products that treat the four diseases separately.

60. The nexus approach was designed to apply a cumulative ratio of qualifying expenditures and overall expenditures, but, as a transitional measure, jurisdictions could allow taxpayers to apply a ratio where qualifying expenditures and overall expenditures were calculated based on a three- or five-year rolling average. Taxpayers would then need to transition from using the three- to five-year average to using a cumulative ratio. An example of how this transition could take place is included in Annex A. Jurisdictions that choose to implement a transitional measure must include anti-avoidance measures to prevent taxpayers from manipulating such a measure. These measures should ensure (i) that taxpayers that previously benefited from a grandfathered regime could not use a transitional measure in a new regime and (ii) that acquisition costs and outsourcing expenditures paid to related parties were included in both the transitional ratio and the cumulative ratio.

61. The nexus approach mandates that jurisdictions include several documentation requirements. Jurisdictions may draft their own specific guidance on these documentation requirements, but they must require at least the following forms of documentation from any taxpayer benefiting from the IP regime:

- If the taxpayer is not tracking directly to the IP asset but is instead tracking to products, the taxpayer must provide documentation showing the complexity of its IP business model and providing justification for using the product-based approach.
- The taxpayer must show that it had a qualifying IP asset (either because the income and expenditures are being tracked to that IP asset or because the product was produced using that IP asset).
- In calculating net IP income, taxpayers must reduce the amount of IP income by any deductions or other tax reductions that arose from the same IP asset (or product). Taxpayers must therefore provide documentation of all relevant deductions and other tax reductions and show why such benefits, if any, were not used to reduce the amount of IP income benefiting from an IP regime.
- Taxpayers that incur expenditures for general or speculative R&D must either show a link between such expenditures and the IP asset or product or provide an explanation for how such expenditures were divided pro rata across IP assets or products.
- The taxpayer must show that both qualifying expenditures and overall expenditures were tracked according to the same IP asset or product as the income and it must provide documentation on this tracking to show that the expenditures and income were linked.
- If the taxpayer acquired an IP asset from a related party, the taxpayer must prepare documentation substantiating the arm's length price. This should include documentation on the overall expenditures that the related party transferor incurred.

I. Grandfathering and safeguards

62. Consistent with the work so far in the area of harmful tax practices, the FHTP agreed in the 2014 Progress Report to draft further guidance on grandfathering, building in particular on paragraph 12 of the 2004 Report (OECD, 2004a), where it says "the Committee decided that where a regime is in the process of being eliminated it shall be treated as abolished … if (1) no new entrants are permitted into the regime, (2) a definite date for complete abolition of the regime has been announced, and (3) the regime is transparent and has effective exchange of information." Jurisdictions have agreed to refrain from adopting new measures that would be inconsistent with the nexus approach or extending the scope of or strengthening existing measures that are inconsistent with the nexus approach.

63. No new entrants will be permitted in any existing IP regime not consistent with the nexus approach after 30 June 2016. If a new regime consistent with the nexus approach takes effect before 30 June 2016, no new entrants will be permitted in the existing IP regime after the new IP regime has taken effect. The FHTP recognised that countries will need time for any legislative process, but it agreed that any legislative process necessary to bring a regime into line with the nexus approach must commence in 2015.

64. For the purposes of grandfathering, "new entrants" include both new taxpayers not previously benefiting from the regime and new IP assets owned by taxpayers already benefiting from the regime. It is understood that taxpayers that may benefit from

grandfathered regimes are only those that fully meet all substantive requirements of the regime and have been officially approved by the tax administration, if required at that point in time. They therefore do not include taxpayers that have only applied for the regime. Taxpayers that have been approved by the tax administration but the IP assets of which have not yet received official approval may, however, benefit from grandfathering if they have applied for IP protection in the jurisdiction of the IP regime but have not yet received official approval because of the length of time of the jurisdiction's approval process.

65. Jurisdictions are also permitted to introduce grandfathering rules that will allow all taxpayers benefiting from an existing regime to keep such entitlement until a second specific date ("abolition date"). The period between the two dates should not exceed 5 years (so the latest possible abolition date would be 30 June 2021). After that date, no more benefits stemming from the respective old regimes may be given to taxpayers.

66. In order to mitigate the risk that new entrants will seek to avail themselves of existing regimes with a view to benefiting from grandfathering, jurisdictions should implement the following safeguards:

- Enhanced transparency for new entrants entering the regime after 6 February 2015 by requiring spontaneous exchange of information on the identity of new entrants benefiting from a grandfathered regime, regardless of whether a ruling is provided, no later than the earlier of (i) three months after the date on which the information becomes available to the competent authority of the jurisdiction providing benefits under the IP regime (and jurisdictions should put in place appropriate systems to ensure that this information is transmitted to the competent authority without undue delay), or (ii) one year after the tax return was filed with the jurisdiction providing benefits under the IP regime.
- Measures that would allow IP assets to benefit from grandfathered regimes not consistent with the nexus approach after 31 December 2016 unless they are acquired directly or indirectly from related parties after 1 January 2016 and they do not qualify for benefits at the time of such acquisition under an existing "back-end" IP regime. Such measures prevent taxpayers that would not otherwise benefit from a grandfathered regime from using related-party acquisitions to shift IP assets into existing regimes in order to take advantage of the grandfathering provision. At the same time, they also permit taxpayers that acquire IP assets from related parties to benefit from grandfathering if this acquisition takes place as part of a domestic or international business restructuring intended to transfer IP assets to regimes that are being modified to comply with the nexus approach.

J. Rebuttable presumption

67. Jurisdictions could treat the nexus ratio as a rebuttable presumption.[21] In the absence of other information from a taxpayer, a jurisdiction would determine the income receiving tax benefits based on the nexus ratio. Taxpayers would, however, have the ability to prove that more income should be permitted to benefit from the IP regime in exceptional circumstances where taxpayers that have undertaken substantial qualifying R&D activity in developing a qualifying IP asset or product can establish that the application of the nexus fraction leads to an outcome where the level of income eligible for a preferential IP regime is not commensurate with the level of their R&D activity. Exceptional circumstances could include, for instance, a complete or partial write down of acquired IP in the taxpayer's financial statements or other instances of an exceptional

nature where a taxpayer can demonstrate that it engaged in greater value creating activity than is reflected in the nexus calculation. If a jurisdiction chooses to treat the nexus ratio as a rebuttable presumption, any adjustments to the nexus ratio must result in outcomes that are commensurate with the level of the taxpayer's R&D activity, consistent with the fundamental principle of the nexus approach. A determination of the application of the rebuttable presumption should be reviewed on an annual basis to determine the continued presence of the exceptional circumstances. Such a review can take the form of a ruling with annual reviews or it can be achieved by other means. In any event, a tax administration must hold contemporaneous documentation showing that the taxpayer has met the requirements set out below in paragraph 68 and any other requirements that may be required under domestic law.

68. A jurisdiction that chooses to treat the nexus ratio as a rebuttable presumption would need to limit the situations where the ratio could be rebutted to those that meet, at a minimum, the following requirements:

- The taxpayer first uses the nexus ratio to establish the presumed amount of income that could qualify for tax benefits.
- The nexus ratio set out above (excluding the up-lift) equals or exceeds 25%.
- The taxpayer demonstrates that because of exceptional circumstances the application of the nexus ratio would result in an outcome that was inconsistent with the principle of the nexus approach. The taxpayer specifies and provides evidence as to the exceptional circumstances.

69. Within these limitations, the design of the rebuttable presumption would be determined by jurisdictions that choose to implement it, but this version of the nexus approach will require greater record-keeping on the part of taxpayers, and jurisdictions would need to establish monitoring procedures and notify the FHTP of the circumstances in which they would allow the nexus ratio to be treated as a rebuttable presumption. Jurisdictions would further need to report on the legal and administrative framework for permitting taxpayers to rebut the nexus ratio, and, on an annual basis, the overall number of companies benefiting from the IP regime, the number of cases in which the rebuttable presumption is used, the number of such cases in which the jurisdiction spontaneously exchanged information, the aggregated value of income receiving benefits under the IP regime (differentiated between income benefiting from the nexus ratio and income benefiting from the rebuttable presumption), and a list of the exceptional circumstances, described in generic terms and without disclosing the identity of the taxpayer, that permitted taxpayers to rebut the nexus ratio in each case. This would permit the FHTP to monitor whether jurisdictions were only permitting taxpayers to rebut the nexus ratio in exceptional circumstances. Regardless of whether taxpayers rebut the nexus ratio in the context of a ruling, jurisdictions would also need to spontaneously exchange, on the basis of information exchange instruments, the contemporaneous documentation it has received from the taxpayer in order to fulfil the requirements for rebutting the nexus ratio set out above. In the context of rulings, jurisdictions would use the framework set out in Chapter 5. Outside the context of rulings, the framework of Chapter 5 would be used to determine the jurisdictions with which to spontaneously exchange such information. A jurisdiction may either exchange the contemporaneous documentation received or may use the template in Annex C and include the information to be exchanged in summary box 7.[22]

III. Substantial activity requirement in the context of non-IP regimes

70. Action 5 requires substantial activity not only for IP regimes but for all preferential regimes. The FHTP has therefore considered the application of the substantial activity requirement to other preferential regimes that have been identified and reviewed by the FHTP since the 1998 Report. A more detailed consideration of how this requirement would apply to specific regimes would need to take place in the context of the specific category of regime being considered. The discussion below sets out the principle that will apply in the context of non-IP regimes.[23]

71. Because IP regimes are designed to encourage R&D activities and contribute to growth and employment, the principle underlying the substantial activity requirement in the context of IP regimes is only to permit taxpayers that did in fact engage in such activities and did incur actual expenditures on such activities to benefit from the regimes. In the context of other preferential regimes, the same principle can also be applied so that such regimes would only be found to meet the substantial activity requirement if they also granted benefits only to qualifying taxpayers[24] to the extent those taxpayers undertook the core income generating activities required to produce the type of business income covered by the preferential regime.

72. When applied to IP regimes, the substantial activity requirement establishes a link between expenditures, IP assets, and IP income. Expenditures are a proxy for activities, and IP assets are used to ensure that the income that receives benefits does in fact arise from the expenditures incurred by the qualifying taxpayer. The effect of this approach is therefore to link income and activities. When applied to other regimes, the substantial activity requirement should also establish a link between the income qualifying for benefits and the core activities necessary to earn the income. As set forth in the 1998 Report, the core activities at issue in non-IP regimes are geographically mobile activities such as financial and other service activities.[25] These activities may not require anything to link them to income because service activities could be seen as contributing directly to the income that receives benefits.

73. The determination of what constitutes the core activities necessary to earn the income depends on the type of regime. Even where regimes are aimed at a similar type of income there can be a wide variation in the application of different countries' regimes, so a more detailed consideration of the relevant core activities would need to be undertaken at the time and in the context of a specific regime being considered. However, a brief description of the type of activities that might be required for the different types of preferential regime is set out below.

A. Headquarters regimes

74. Headquarters regimes grant preferential tax treatment to taxpayers that provide certain services such as managing, co-ordinating or controlling business activities for a group as a whole or for group members in a specific geographical area. These regimes may raise concerns about ring-fencing or because they provide for an artificial definition of the tax base where the profits of an entity are determined based on a "cost-plus" basis but certain costs are excluded from the basis or particular circumstances are not taken into account. These features could be addressed by the existing factors, but these regimes could also raise concerns in respect of substance.

75. The core income-generating activities in a headquarters company could include the key activities giving rise to the particular type of services income received by the

company. For example, they could include taking relevant management decisions, incurring expenditures on behalf of group entities, and co-ordinating group activities.

B. Distribution and service centre regimes

76. Distribution centre regimes provide preferential tax treatment to entities whose main or only activity is to purchase raw materials and finished products from other group members and re-sell them for a small percentage of profits. Service centre regimes provide preferential tax treatment to entities whose main or only activity is to provide services to other entities of the same group. A concern with such regimes is that they may have ring-fencing features. In addition, they may raise concerns that they permit an artificial definition of the tax base. Although these concerns may be addressed through the existing factors, concerns with respect to substance could remain.

77. The core income-generating activities in a distribution or service centre company could include activities such as transporting and storing goods; managing the stocks and taking orders; and providing consulting or other administrative services.

C. Financing or leasing regimes

78. Financing and leasing regimes are regimes which provide a preferential tax treatment to financing and leasing activities. The main concerns underlying these regimes include, among others, ring-fencing considerations and an artificial definition of the tax base. Again, those concerns could be addressed through the existing factors.

79. The core income-generating activities in a financing or leasing company could include agreeing funding terms; identifying and acquiring assets to be leased (in the case of leasing); setting the terms and duration of any financing or leasing; monitoring and revising any agreements; and managing any risks.

D. Fund management regimes

80. Fund management regimes grant preferential tax treatment to income earned by fund managers[26] for the management of funds. In exchange for its services, the fund manager receives compensation that is computed on the basis of a pre-agreed formula. The focus is not the taxation of the income or gains of the fund itself or of the investors in a fund but the income earned by fund managers from the management of the fund.[27] The remuneration of the fund manager and how and where this is taxed may raise issues of transparency and these could in part be dealt with by the compulsory spontaneous exchange of rulings.

81. In terms of substantial activity the core income-generating activities for a fund manager could include taking decisions on the holding and selling of investments; calculating risks and reserves; taking decisions on currency or interest fluctuations and hedging positions; and preparing relevant regulatory or other reports for government authorities and investors.

E. Banking and insurance regimes

82. Banking and insurance regimes provide preferential tax treatment to banking and insurance activities. The main concern is linked to the benefits that they provide to income from foreign activities. If benefits are only provided to foreign income, then this could be addressed through the existing ring-fencing factor. In terms of substance, the regulatory environment, where applicable, should already ensure that a business is

capable of bearing risk and undertaking its activity. However, in the context of insurance, it may be more difficult to easily identify those activities and regimes that raise concerns in respect of substance versus those that do not because of the possibility that risks may have been re-insured.

83. The core income-generating activities for banking companies depend on the type of banking activity undertaken, but they could include raising funds; managing risk including credit, currency and interest risk; taking hedging positions; providing loans, credit or other financial services to customers; managing regulatory capital; and preparing regulatory reports and returns. The core income-generating activities for insurance companies could include predicting and calculating risk, insuring or re-insuring against risk, and providing client services.

F. Shipping regimes

84. Shipping regimes provide a preferential tax treatment to shipping activities and are designed taking into considerations significant non-tax considerations. In addition to issues of ring-fencing and transparency already discussed in the CAN (OECD, 2004b), they may also raise concerns under the substantial activity analysis where they permit the separation of shipping income from the core activities that generate it.

85. The core income-generating activities for shipping companies could include managing the crew (including hiring, paying, and overseeing crewmembers); hauling and maintaining ships; overseeing and tracking deliveries; determining what goods to order and when to deliver them; and organising and overseeing voyages.

G. Holding company regimes

86. Holding company regimes can be broadly divided into two categories: (i) those that provide benefits to companies that hold a variety of assets and earn different types of income (e.g. interest, rents, and royalties) and (ii) those that apply only to companies that hold equity participations and earn only dividends and capital gains. In the context of (i) above, to the extent that holding company regimes provide benefits to companies that earn income other than dividends and capital gains, the substantial activity requirement should require qualifying taxpayers to have engaged in the core activities associated with those types of income.

87. Holding companies that fall within category (ii) above and that provide benefits only to dividends and capital gains, however, raise different policy considerations than other preferential regimes in that they primarily focus on alleviating economic double taxation. They therefore may not in fact require much substance in order to exercise their main activity of holding and managing equity participations. These regimes could, however, raise policy concerns that are not directly related to substance. Countries' concerns about holding company regimes are often related to transparency and their inability to identify the beneficial owner of the dividends. Related concerns include whether holding companies enable the payer and payee to benefit from treaty benefits in circumstances that would not otherwise qualify for benefits and whether holding company regimes are ring-fenced. Some of these concerns may already be addressed in other work or under other existing factors. For instance:

- Exchange of Information: The international standard on information exchange upon request covers not only the exchange of information but also the availability of information, including ownership, banking, and account information. The work on monitoring this standard is carried out by the Global Forum on Transparency and Exchange of Information on Tax Purposes. Under its revised terms of reference, the Global Forum has incorporated the principles of the Financial Action Task Force (FATF) standard of beneficial ownership and as a result countries will be assessed on their ability to provide information on beneficial ownership where relevant and where this forms part of a request for exchange of information.

- Action 6 to prevent treaty abuse: The result of this Action takes the form of new model treaty provisions and recommendations regarding the design of domestic rules to prevent the granting of treaty benefits in inappropriate circumstances. The work done under this Action should address concerns about the use of holding companies to receive treaty benefits.
- Action 2 to neutralise the effects of hybrid mismatch arrangements: The result of this Action takes the form of new model treaty provisions and recommendations regarding the design of domestic rules to neutralise the effect of hybrid instruments and entities. The work done under this Action has led to a recommendation to deny a dividend exemption and other types of relief granted to relieve economic double taxation on deductible payments. This could again address some of the concern that "dividend" income can go untaxed.
- Ring-fencing: If countries are concerned that equity holding companies are providing benefits to income only from foreign companies and that this income is not already taxed anywhere or the regime is otherwise targeting foreign investors, this concern is already addressed under the existing ring-fencing factor.[28]
- Other work: Such as the work done under Action 3 of the BEPS Action Plan to strengthen controlled foreign company (CFC) rules.

88. Once these other policy considerations have been addressed, there should be less of a concern that these regimes are used for BEPS. Therefore, to the extent that holding company regimes provide benefits only to equity holding companies, the substantial activity factor requires, at a minimum, that the companies receiving benefits from such regimes respect all applicable corporate law filing requirements and have the substance necessary to engage in holding and managing equity participations (for example, by showing that they have both the people and the premises necessary for these activities). This precludes the possibility of letter box and brass plate companies from benefiting from holding company regimes.

Notes

1. See p. 17 of the BEPS Action Plan. See also Chapter 1 above.

2. For details on the agreement, see *Action 5: Agreement on Modified Nexus Approach for IP Regimes* (OECD, 2015).

3. For example, Company A, Company B, and Company C together develop IP Asset D in Year 1. Company A is in a jurisdiction with an IP regime. Company A contributes 30% of the R&D and 3 000 of the R&D funding, Company B contributes 30% of the R&D and 3 000 of the R&D funding, and Company C contributes 40% of the R&D and 4 000 of the R&D funding. IP Asset D produces 100 000 of IP income in Year 2, and 30 000 of this IP income is allocated to Company A. If Company A did not pay to outsource to a related company or to acquire any IP assets, then the nexus ratio that would apply to that 30 000 before the up-lift is 3 000/3 000 (or 100%). The entire 30 000 would therefore qualify for the IP regime in Company A's jurisdiction.

4. Jurisdictions with IP regimes should ensure that the same IP asset is not allocated to both the head office and the foreign PE (e.g. because they apply the authorised OECD approach (AOA)).

5. For this purpose, legal protection includes exclusive rights to use the IP asset, legal remedies against infringement, trade secret law, and contractual and criminal protections against use of the IP asset or unauthorised disclosure of information related to the IP asset.

6. Although some jurisdictions provide patent protection for software, not all jurisdictions do so. Many taxpayers that produce software must therefore copyright it instead of relying on patent protection. Including copyrighted software in the definition of functionally equivalent IP assets also ensures that the different treatment of software under the patent laws of different jurisdictions does not affect whether or not income from software could benefit from IP regimes.

7. The determination of whether a taxpayer meets these two requirements should be made on an annual basis, using a five-year average that changes every year. The reference to EUR 50 million in global group-wide turnover does not mean that these requirements only apply to groups. Stand-alone entities that want to qualify for benefits using the third category of IP assets must also meet these two requirements.

8. The information on the use of the third category of IP assets would then be included in the summary box 7 of the template set out in Annex C.

9. IP regimes that must be assessed under the nexus approach include regimes that grant benefits to *any* IP assets. Regimes that grant benefits to IP assets that are not qualifying IP assets for purposes of the nexus approach would be found not to meet the substantial activity requirement.

10. Qualifying expenditures could therefore include salary and wages, direct costs, overhead costs directly associated with R&D facilities, and cost of supplies so long as all of these costs arise out of activities undertaken to advance the understanding of

scientific relations or technologies, address known scientific or technological obstacles, or otherwise increase knowledge or develop new applications.

11. Building costs or other non-separable capital costs would not be included because it would be impossible to establish a direct link between the cost of an entire building and different IP assets created in that building.

12. See Sections II.F and II.G of this Chapter for an explanation of why expenditures for related-party outsourcing and acquisition costs are included in overall expenditures and not in qualifying expenditures.

13. See Section II.E of this Chapter below.

14. IP expenditures will be calculated by applying the ordinary domestic tax law provisions (i.e. not using specific provisions in IP regimes). Jurisdictions may limit expenditures allocable to IP income to ensure that the use of such expenditures is consistent with domestic legislation. Jurisdictions should also use any tax losses associated with the IP income in a manner that is consistent with domestic legislation and that does not allow the diversion of those losses against income that is taxed at the ordinary rate.

15. Such a method would need to be based on transfer pricing principles as updated through the report on Actions 8-10 of the BEPS Action Plan.

16. Jurisdictions that are not Member States of the European Union (EU) could modify this limitation to include all qualifying expenditures for activities undertaken by both unrelated parties and resident related parties in the definition of qualifying expenditures.

17. Outsourcing is different from the buying in of components from a party that owns the IP to those components, and this reference to the likelihood of outsourcing to unrelated parties does not refer to the likelihood of buying components from unrelated parties.

18. Jurisdictions with IP regimes need to ensure that taxpayers are not able to circumvent this treatment of acquisition costs by acquiring entities that own IP assets.

19. Jurisdictions that are not Member States of the EU could modify this limitation so that the acquisition of a taxpayer that incurred qualifying expenditures in the jurisdiction providing the IP regime allowed those expenditures to be included in the qualifying expenditures of the acquirer (while either including the acquisition costs in overall expenditures or including all the overall expenditures of the transferor in the overall expenditures of the acquirer if the transferor has engaged in complete tracking and tracing to ensure that all overall expenditures are included).

20. Therapeutic or therapy areas include classes of diseases, such as cardiology, oncology, or respiratory diseases. Narrower disease categories would be subsets of therapeutic areas, such as breast cancer and lung cancer instead of the broader therapeutic area of oncology.

In certain industries that produce services or other outputs other than products, product families could include functional equivalents as long as these groupings include only those IP assets that arose from overlapping expenditures and contributed to overlapping streams of income.

21. Taxpayers in jurisdictions that treat the nexus ratio as a rebuttable presumption would have to choose between the up-lift and the rebuttable presumption. In other words, taxpayers could not both rebut the nexus ratio and benefit from the 30% up-lift.

Taxpayers must choose between the up-lift and rebutting the nexus ratio on the basis of IP asset, product, or product family, and taxpayers may not choose based on a narrower grouping than that used for tracking and tracing.

22. Any further information could be requested on the basis of applicable information exchange instruments.

23. These regimes include (i) holding company regimes, (ii) headquarters regimes, (iii) distribution centre regimes, (iv) service centre regimes, (v) financing and leasing regimes, (vi) fund management regimes, (vii) banking regimes, (viii) insurance regimes and (ix) shipping company regimes.

24. "Qualifying taxpayers" would have the same definition as that set out in the context of IP regimes. See paragraph 33 above. This definition includes resident companies, domestic PEs of foreign companies, and foreign PEs of resident companies that are subject to tax in the jurisdiction providing benefits.

25. See paragraph 6 of 1998 Report, p. 8.

26. A fund manager is a legal or natural person that provides management services, including making decisions on investments, to an investment fund or its investors.

27. See paragraph 261 of the CAN, p. 73. The work of the FHTP is focused on fund management and not the taxation of the fund itself.

28. According to paragraph 65 of the CAN, p. 21, the ring-fencing factor is not implicated in connection with measures designed to eliminate or mitigate double taxation but "it must have some features to ensure that it only applies where double taxation may arise." In the context of holding company regimes paragraph 244 of the CAN, pp. 68-69, adds that:

> … the holding company regime must, therefore, provide for the operation of effective measures to achieve this objective. Such measures may include, for instance, subject to tax clauses, controlled foreign company legislation (or similar rules that apply at the time of distribution of dividends or disposition of shares), the use of exemptions methods in the context of income tax conventions following the OECD Model Convention with Respect to Taxes on Income and on Capital (hereafter the "OECD Model Tax Convention"), or the use of anti-abuse measures. (OECD, 2004b)

Bibliography

OECD (2015), *Action 5: Agreement on Modified Nexus Approach for IP Regimes*, OECD, www.oecd.org/ctp/beps-action-5-agreement-on-modified-nexus-approach-for-ip-regimes.pdf.

OECD (2014), *Countering Harmful Tax Practices More Effectively, Taking into Account Transparency and Substance*, OECD Publishing, Paris, http://dx.doi.org/10.1787/9789264218970-en.

OECD (2013), *Action Plan on Base Erosion and Profit Shifting*, OECD Publishing, Paris, http://dx.doi.org/10.1787/9789264202719-en.

OECD (2004a), *Harmful Tax Practices: The 2004 Progress Report,* OECD, www.oecd.org/ctp/harmful/30901115.pdf.

OECD (2004b), *Consolidated Application Note: Guidance in Applying the 1998 Report to Preferential Tax Regimes*, OECD, www.oecd.org/ctp/harmful/30901132.pdf.

OECD (1998), *Harmful Tax Competition: An Emerging Global Issue*, OECD Publishing, Paris, http://dx.doi.org/10.1787/9789264162945-en.

Chapter 5

Revamp of the work on harmful tax practices: Framework for improving transparency in relation to rulings

I. Introduction

89. The second priority under Action 5 for revamping the work on harmful tax practices is to improve transparency, including the compulsory spontaneous exchange of information on certain rulings. This work contributes to the third pillar of the BEPS Project which has the objective of ensuring transparency while promoting increased certainty and predictability.

90. The FHTP decided to take forward the work on improving transparency in three steps:

a) The first step focused on developing a framework for compulsory spontaneous information exchange in respect of rulings related to preferential regimes. This framework was set out in the FHTP's 2014 Progress Report (OECD, 2014a) and has been modified, and it is now superseded by the guidance in this report. The 2014 Progress Report made it clear that the framework would be dynamic and flexible and that further work would be undertaken.

b) In the second step of the work, the FHTP has considered whether transparency can be further improved and has considered the ruling regimes in OECD and associate countries. This work, which included a questionnaire completed by OECD and associate countries on existing ruling practices, has informed further developments of the framework on the compulsory spontaneous exchange of information. It has led to the conclusion that the requirement to undertake compulsory spontaneous information exchange should generally cover all instances in which the absence of exchange of a ruling may give rise to BEPS concerns. This approach builds on the fact that Action 5 is not limited to exchanging information on rulings related to preferential regimes but allows for broader transparency. In this context, the FHTP focuses on specific instances where the absence of exchanges can cause BEPS concerns rather than suggesting that in all such instances the country providing the ruling operates a preferential regime. This also reflects the fact that a meaningful transparency discipline may have to go wider than the related substantive discipline. For instance, there is no suggestion that a unilateral advance pricing arrangements (APAs) program is by itself a preferential regime. However, a preferential regime, especially one of an administrative nature, may be operated, in whole or in part, via an APA or advance tax ruling (ATR) regime. In such cases, it is only once information on the ruling is exchanged that a fully informed decision can be made. Rather than engaging in a line drawing exercise that would have been very challenging in practice and would have put the issuing tax administration in the difficult position of having to determine the nature of its own regime, the FHTP opted for simplicity and clarity. In so doing, the FHTP also noted that under Action 13 on transfer pricing documentation APAs and ATRs are to be included in the local and the master file and felt that the spontaneous exchange of key information on such APAs and ATRs between tax administrations would provide a useful cross-check with the information provided by the taxpayer.

c) In a third step, the FHTP developed a general best practices framework for the design and operation of ruling regimes.

91. Combining the first and the second steps described above, this Chapter sets out the agreed OECD framework for the compulsory spontaneous exchange of information in respect of rulings. This includes six categories of taxpayer-specific rulings which in the absence of compulsory spontaneous exchange of information could give rise to BEPS concerns. These six categories are (i) rulings relating to preferential regimes; (ii) unilateral APAs or other cross-border unilateral rulings in respect of transfer pricing; (iii) cross-border rulings providing for a downward adjustment of taxable profits; (iv) permanent establishment (PE) rulings; (v) related party conduit rulings; and (vi) any other type of ruling agreed by the FHTP that in the absence of spontaneous information exchange gives rise to BEPS concerns. This does not mean that such rulings or the legal or administrative procedures under which they are given represent preferential regimes. Instead it reflects countries' concerns that a lack of transparency can lead to BEPS, if countries have no knowledge or information on the tax treatment of a taxpayer in a specific country and that tax treatment affects the transactions or arrangements undertaken with a related taxpayer resident in their country. The availability of timely and targeted information, contained in a template discussed below in Section V of this Chapter and Annex C, is essential to enable tax administrations to quickly identify risk areas.

92. The framework was designed with a view to finding a balance between ensuring that the information exchanged is relevant to other tax administrations and that it does not impose an unnecessary administrative burden on either the country exchanging the information or the country receiving it. The framework builds on the guidance contained in the CAN (OECD, 2004) and also takes into account the Convention on Mutual Administrative Assistance in Tax Matters (MAC, OECD, 2010a)[1] and the European Union's Council Directive 2011/16/EU of 15 February 2011 on administrative cooperation in the field of taxation (including its work on spontaneous information exchange in the context of transfer pricing and cross-border rulings). These sources all have a common goal in that they seek to encourage spontaneous information exchange in circumstances where it is assumed that information obtained by one country will be of interest to another country.

93. Whilst it is recognised that rulings are a useful tool for both tax administrations and taxpayers, providing for certainty and predictability and thus avoiding tax disputes from even arising, concerns over transparency are not new and ruling regimes have been an area of focus since the start of the OECD's work on harmful tax practices. There is extensive guidance in the CAN on transparency. As the 1998 Report (OECD, 1998) and the CAN make clear, transparency is often relevant in connection with rulings, including unilateral APAs and administrative practices more widely, where spontaneous notification may be required. Ruling regimes can also be used to attract internationally

mobile capital to a jurisdiction and they have the potential to do this in a manner that contributes to, or constitutes, a harmful tax practice.

94. This Chapter deals with the following: (i) which rulings are covered; (ii) which countries information needs to be exchanged with; (iii) application of the framework to past and future rulings; (iv) information subject to the exchange; (v) practical implementation issues; (vi) reciprocal approach to exchange of information; (vii) confidentiality of the information exchanged; and (viii) recommendations on best practices in respect of rulings.

II. Rulings covered by the spontaneous exchange framework

A. Definition of a ruling

95. Rulings are "any advice, information or undertaking provided by a tax authority to a specific taxpayer or group of taxpayers concerning their tax situation and on which they are entitled to rely."[2]

96. Whilst the terms of a ruling may be relied upon by the taxpayer, this is typically subject to the condition that the facts on which the ruling is based have been accurately presented and that the taxpayer abides by the terms of the ruling. This definition is wide and includes both general rulings and taxpayer-specific rulings. However, the framework for compulsory spontaneous exchange of information only applies to taxpayer-specific rulings.

97. *Taxpayer-specific rulings* are rulings that apply to a specific taxpayer and on which that taxpayer is entitled to rely. Such rulings can be given both pre-transaction (this includes ATRs or clearances and APAs) and post-transaction, in each case in response to a ruling request by the taxpayer. The definition of rulings therefore excludes, for example, any statement or agreement reached as a result of an audit carried out after a taxpayer has filed its tax return or accounts. This does not however, exclude any ruling or agreement, on the treatment of future profits, given as a result of an audit if that ruling falls within any of the categories set out in this report.

98. *Advance tax rulings* are specific to an individual taxpayer and provide a determination of the tax consequences of a proposed transaction on which the particular taxpayer is entitled to rely. Advance tax rulings may come in a variety of forms and may include rulings or clearances that are given as part of a statutory process or an administrative practice, including rulings that are given informally. They frequently determine whether, and in some cases how, particular law and administrative practice will be applicable to a proposed transaction undertaken by a specific taxpayer. Such rulings may also provide a determination of whether or how a general ruling applies to the facts and circumstances of a particular taxpayer. Typically, the taxpayer concerned will make an application for a ruling before undertaking the transaction concerned, although some regimes provide guidance to taxpayers after a transaction has been carried out and these post-transaction rulings will also be covered. The ruling will provide a determination of the tax consequences of the relevant transaction on which the taxpayer is entitled to rely, assuming that the facts are as described in the advance tax ruling request. Such rulings are tailor-made for the taxpayer concerned as they take into account the factual situation of the taxpayer and are thus not directly applicable to other taxpayers (although, when published in anonymised or redacted form, such rulings may provide guidance to taxpayers with similar facts and circumstances[3]). This category of rulings could include, for example, rulings on transfer pricing matters that fall short of an advance pricing

arrangement. It may also include a view or determination of the future tax treatment of the taxpayer on which they are entitled to rely.

99. *Advance pricing arrangements* are defined in the OECD Transfer Pricing Guidelines for Multinational Enterprises and Tax Administrations (TP Guidelines, OECD, 2010b) as "an arrangement that determines, in advance of controlled transactions, an appropriate set of criteria ... for the determination of the transfer pricing for those transactions over a fixed period of time."[4] They provide taxpayers with certainty about how transfer pricing rules apply to future transactions within the scope of the APA. They normally do this by determining an appropriate set of criteria (e.g. method, comparables and appropriate adjustments thereto and critical assumptions as to future events) for the determination of the transfer pricing.[5]

100. The TP Guidelines distinguish APAs from other rulings procedures, such as advance tax rulings, in the following way:

> *The APA differs from the classic ruling procedure, in that it requires the detailed review and to the extent appropriate, verification of the factual assumptions on which the determination of legal consequences is based, before any such determinations can be made. Further the APA provides for a continual monitoring of whether the factual assumptions remain valid throughout the course of the APA period.* (OECD, 2010b)[6]

101. APAs may be unilateral, bilateral or multilateral. Bilateral and multilateral APAs are concluded between two or more tax authorities under the mutual agreement procedure of the applicable tax treaties. Typically, the associated enterprises applying for an APA provide documentation to the tax authorities concerning the industry, markets and countries to be covered by the agreement, together with details of their proposed methodology, any transactions that may serve as comparables, and a functional analysis of the contribution of each of the relevant enterprises. Because APAs govern the methodology for the determination of transfer prices for future years, they necessitate assumptions or predictions about future events.

102. *General rulings* apply to groups or types of taxpayers or may be given in relation to a defined set of circumstances or activities, rather than applying to a specific taxpayer. They typically provide guidance on the position of the tax authority on such matters as the interpretation of law and administrative practice[7] and on their application to taxpayers generally, to a specified group of taxpayers or to specified activities. This guidance typically applies to all taxpayers that engage in activities or undertake transactions that fall within the scope of the ruling. Such rulings are often published and can be applied by taxpayers to their relevant activities or transactions without them needing to make an application for a specific ruling. The framework does not apply to general rulings but the best practices do apply.

B. Taxpayer-specific rulings related to preferential regimes

103. The FHTP has already agreed to a framework, described in the FHTP's 2014 Progress Report in respect of the compulsory exchange of information on rulings related to preferential regimes. A filter approach is used for such rulings so that there is an obligation to spontaneously exchange information on cross-border taxpayer-specific rulings related to regimes that (i) are within the scope of the work of FHTP; (ii) are preferential; and (iii) meet the low or no effective tax rate factor.[8] Where rulings are given

in respect of these regimes there will be an obligation to spontaneously exchange information.

104. The obligation to spontaneously exchange information arises for rulings related to *any* such preferential regime. That is, a regime does not need to have been reviewed or found to be potentially or actually harmful within the meaning of the 1998 Report for the obligation to arise. Therefore, the obligation will also apply to any ruling (as defined) in connection with preferential regimes that have not yet been reviewed or that have been reviewed but that have not been found to be potentially or actually harmful and that have therefore been cleared.

105. Countries that have preferential regimes that have not yet been reviewed by the FHTP will need to self-assess and take a view on whether the filters are satisfied. Where this is the case, the obligation to spontaneously exchange information arises immediately, without the FHTP first needing to formally review the relevant regime. In case of doubt as to the applicability of the filters, it is recommended that the relevant country spontaneously exchange information. The expectation is that a country that has a preferential regime which has not yet been reviewed by the FHTP will in the meantime self-refer this regime for review by the FHTP.

106. As the framework now includes six categories of rulings some of the procedures that were described in the FHTP's 2014 Progress Report have been modified and simplified and this report supersedes the 2014 Progress Report.

C. Cross-border unilateral APAs and any other cross-border unilateral tax rulings (such as ATRs) covering transfer pricing or the application of transfer pricing principles

107. Unilateral APAs are APAs established between a tax administration of one country and a taxpayer in its country.

108. "Other cross-border unilateral tax rulings covering transfer pricing or the application of transfer pricing principles" cover, for example, ATRs on transfer pricing issues that fall short of an APA, for instance, because the ruling is limited to addressing questions of a legal nature based on facts presented by a taxpayer (unlike an APA which generally deals with factual issues) or because the ruling is binding only for a particular transaction (unlike an APA, which usually covers several transactions, several types of transactions on a continuing basis, or all of a taxpayer's international transactions for a given period of time).

109. Unilateral APAs and other unilateral tax rulings are in the scope of covered rulings, not because they are preferential but because, in the absence of transparency, they can create distortions and may give rise to BEPS concerns and either directly or indirectly impact on the tax position in another country. In some countries, unilateral APAs can adjust profits both upwards and downwards from the starting position. In addition unilateral APAs can set a future transfer pricing methodology or a future pricing or profit apportionment structure. If the terms of such agreements are not available to the tax administrations dealing with related taxpayers then there can be mismatches in how two ends of a transaction are priced and taxed with the result that profits go untaxed resulting in base erosion or profit shifting concerns.

110. There is an interaction between the obligation to spontaneously exchange information on this category of rulings and the transfer pricing documentation requirements under Action 13. In particular, the master file will contain a list and brief

description of the MNE group's existing unilateral APAs and other tax rulings relating to the allocation of income among countries. The local file will contain a copy of existing unilateral and bilateral/multilateral APAs and other tax rulings to which the local jurisdiction is not a party and which are related to the relevant material controlled transactions.

111. However, the obligation to spontaneously exchange information on unilateral APAs and other transfer pricing rulings could potentially cover a wider range of transfer pricing rulings than those captured in the local file and the master file. For example, only rulings related to "relevant material controlled transactions" will be contained in the local file which creates a higher threshold than that required under Action 5. Also, certain information in the local file may be subject to local materiality thresholds so certain taxpayers may not be required to produce a local file.

112. Lastly, those two sets of obligations are mutually reinforcing, allowing tax administrations to cross-check the information reported by taxpayers against the information exchanged from another tax administration and vice versa. This dual requirement may also give rise to additional information which could help tax administrations identify cases where they want to formulate a request for an additional exchange of information with another tax authority.

D. Cross-border rulings providing for a unilateral downward adjustment to the taxpayer's taxable profits that is not directly reflected in the taxpayer's financial/commercial accounts

113. This covers, for example, informal capital or similar rulings, to the extent not already covered by Section II.C above. The CAN specifically refers to advance tax rulings or unilateral APAs providing for a downward adjustment that is not reflected in the company's financial accounts as being examples that could result in a lack of transparency where the tax authority does not notify the other tax authority of the existence of the ruling. Moreover, the 2000 Report (OECD, 2001) recognised that regimes that allow negative adjustments to profits could be preferential regimes.[9]

114. A regime that provides for negative adjustments to profits has the potential to result in no or low taxation and MNEs have the incentive to shift profits. This incentive exists where the downward adjustment is predictable, for example, where it is part of a ruling or other administrative practice. In such cases, effective exchange of information is particularly important in order to give other countries the opportunity to apply their transfer pricing rules. In many cases the affected country will not be able to determine that such an adjustment has been made because, for example, the adjustment is made in a domestic tax computation without being reflected in an enterprise's accounts or it is made retrospectively.[10]

115. Excess profits rulings, informal capital rulings and other similar rulings recognise the contribution of capital or an asset, generally by the parent company or another related party, and provide an adjustment that reduces the taxable profits, for instance, through a deemed interest deduction in the case of an interest free loan. An example of this would be where the price paid by a subsidiary to its parent company is stated to be lower than the arm's length price and this is done intentionally to favour the subsidiary. In such circumstances a country may make a downward adjustment to the subsidiary's taxable profits to reflect the price that it would have paid had the transaction been undertaken at arm's length. The downward adjustment will reflect the difference between the actual price paid and the arm's length price so that in the company's tax computations (but not

in the company's commercial/statutory accounts), the difference will be treated as having been paid by the subsidiary to its parent. This will create a tax deduction and reduce the subsidiary's effective tax rate, but there is unlikely to be any corresponding additional taxation in the parent company jurisdiction unless it is aware of the adjustment and its amount. Further, it has been agreed that countries where an informal capital contribution or excess profits regime can lead to downward adjustments and that do not require taxpayers to obtain a ruling to benefit from this regime, will ensure that the tax administration is aware of all cases where the regime has been utilised. Information on those cases will also be provided to other relevant tax authorities.

116. This category of ruling is neither intended to cover downward adjustments made following audits of filed accounts and returns where there is no separate ruling nor unilateral relief for items such as foreign tax credits.

E. Permanent establishment (PE) rulings, i.e. rulings concerning the existence or absence of, and/or the attribution of profits to, a permanent establishment by the country giving the ruling

117. This covers rulings, to the extent not already covered by Section II.C above, which explicitly determine or decide on the existence or absence of a PE (either inside or outside of the country giving the ruling) or any ruling that provides for how much profit will be attributed to a PE.

F. Related party conduit rulings

118. To the extent not already covered by Section II.C above, this includes rulings, covering arrangements involving cross-border flows of funds or income through an entity in the country giving the ruling, whether those funds or income flow to another country directly or indirectly (i.e. through another domestic entity first).

119. Indirect conduit arrangements include, for example, arrangements whereby a lower tier domestic entity receives cross-border income payments (i.e. an interest payment on a loan) from underlying operating companies, which it then pays to a higher tier domestic entity as an interest payment on a loan, leaving a small taxable margin in the lower tier entity. The higher tier entity is treated as a tax transparent entity under domestic law and only has non-resident partners thereby avoiding taxation. The effect of this is an interest deduction in the underlying operating companies with no corresponding income pick-up in domestic entities (except the small margin) or in the non-resident partners.

G. Any other type of ruling that in the absence of spontaneous information exchange gives rise to BEPS concerns

120. If at a later date, the FHTP agrees, this category could be used for any other type of ruling that, in the absence of compulsory spontaneous exchange of information, gives rise to BEPS concerns. This language is intended to give the FHTP flexibility in the future to broaden the obligation to spontaneously exchange to additional categories of rulings. This would only therefore apply where the FHTP subsequently agrees that other rulings give rise to similar concerns as the rulings already included within the framework and should therefore be added.

III. Jurisdictions receiving the information

121. As a general rule, exchange of information on rulings for the six categories need to take place with:

a) The countries of residence of all related parties with which the taxpayer enters into a transaction for which a ruling is granted or which gives rise to income from related parties benefiting from a preferential treatment (this rule also applies in a PE context); and

b) The residence country of the ultimate parent company and the immediate parent company.

122. The related party threshold has been set at 25% but the FHTP agreed that this is to be kept under review. Accordingly, two parties would be considered related if the first person has a 25% or greater investment in the second person or there is a third person that holds a 25% or greater investment in both. A person will be treated as holding a percentage investment in another person if that person holds directly or indirectly through an investment in other persons, a percentage of the voting rights of that person or of the value of any equity interests of that person.

123. The general two-part rule above applies in the case of (i) shipping company regimes; (ii) banking regimes; (iii) insurance regimes; (iv) financing and leasing regimes; (v) fund management regimes; (vi) headquarters regimes; (vii) distribution centre regimes; (viii) service centre regimes; (ix) IP regimes; (x) holding company regimes; and (xi) other miscellaneous regimes identified as preferential regimes by the FHTP.

124. The same two-part exchange rule applies for (i) cross-border unilateral APAs and any other cross-border unilateral tax rulings and (ii) cross-border rulings providing for a unilateral downward adjustment. For PE rulings, the information is exchanged with the residence country of the head office, or the country of the PE, as the case may be, and the residence country of the ultimate parent company and the immediate parent company. For conduit rulings, the information is exchanged with (i) the country of residence of any related party making payments to the conduit (directly or indirectly); (ii) the country of residence of the ultimate beneficial owner (which in most cases will be the ultimate parent company) of payments made to the conduit; and (iii) to the extent not already covered by (ii), the residence country of (a) the ultimate parent company and (b) the immediate parent company.

125. The table below summarises the countries with which information should be exchanged, with respect to all the rulings discussed above. The first column of the table describes what rulings are covered by the obligation to spontaneously exchange and the second column sets out with which countries information needs to be exchanged.

Table 5.1 Summary of the countries with which information should be exchanged

What rulings are covered?	With which country does information need to be exchanged?
1. Rulings related to a preferential regime **Shipping company regimes, banking regimes, insurance regimes, financing and leasing regimes, fund management regimes, headquarters regimes, distribution centre regimes, service centre regimes, IP regimes, holding company regimes, and other miscellaneous regimes identified as preferential regimes by the FHTP**	i. The countries of residence of all related parties (a 25% threshold would apply), with which the taxpayer enters into a transaction for which a preferential treatment is granted or which gives rise to income from related parties benefiting from a preferential treatment (this rule also applies in a PE context); and ii. The residence country of (a) the ultimate parent company and (b) the immediate parent company.
2. Cross-border unilateral APAs and any other cross-border unilateral tax ruling (such as an ATR) covering transfer pricing or the application of transfer pricing principles	i. The countries of residence of all related parties with whom the taxpayer enters into transactions that are covered by the APA or cross-border unilateral tax ruling; and ii. The residence country of (a) the ultimate parent company and (b) the immediate parent company.
3. Cross-border rulings giving a unilateral downward adjustment to the taxpayer's taxable profits in the country giving the ruling	i. The countries of residence of all related parties with whom the taxpayer enters into transactions covered by the ruling. ii. The residence country of (a) the ultimate parent company and (b) the immediate parent company
4. PE rulings	i. The residence country of the head office, or the country of the PE, as the case may be; and ii. The residence country of (a) the ultimate parent company and (b) the immediate parent company.
5. Related party conduit rulings	i. The country of residence of any related party making payments to the conduit (directly or indirectly); ii. The country of residence of the ultimate beneficial owner (which in most cases will be the ultimate parent company) of payments made to the conduit; and iii. To the extent not already covered by ii), the residence country of (a) the ultimate parent company and (b) the immediate parent company.

IV. Application of the framework to rulings[11]

Past rulings

126. The obligation to spontaneously exchange applies not only to *future rulings*, but also to *past rulings* that relate to earlier years. It has been agreed that information on rulings that have been issued on or after 1 January 2010 and were still in effect as from 1 January 2014 must be exchanged.

127. In order to exchange with the relevant countries identified in Section III above, jurisdictions will need to be able to identify related parties, the ultimate parent, the immediate parent, and/or the ultimate beneficial owner, as the case may be. For past rulings there will be many cases (such as unilateral APAs and other cross-border transfer

pricing rulings) where much of the information, especially in relation to related parties, is available. Also, information on immediate and ultimate parent entities will typically be in the possession of the tax administration. However, this may not be the case in respect of all relevant related parties, for instance, in connection with rulings relating to IP regimes, or where an APA has focused on the transfer pricing methodology rather than specific transactions. In these cases, countries may not have routinely identified related parties who undertake transactions.

128. Where a ruling does not contain sufficient information to enable identification of all the relevant countries with which the information needs to be exchanged, a country is not expected to contact the taxpayer but can instead use "best efforts" to identify the countries with which to exchange information on the ruling. This requires a tax administration to check the information that it has in its possession, for instance, in the rulings or the wider taxpayer file, including any relevant transfer pricing documentation. Where such information is not already in the possession of the tax administration but is available from sources easily accessible to the tax administration (e.g. a corporate registry system) tax administrations would be expected to extend their efforts to such sources.

Future rulings

129. For future rulings, countries will need to take the necessary measures to ensure they have, or are able to obtain, information that identifies the countries they must exchange with. For future rulings, this may mean that countries will need to amend their ruling practices to require taxpayers to provide that information as part of the ruling process. Given that countries that issue rulings covered by this report may need to amend their ruling practices, future rulings will only be those issued on or after 1 April 2016.

V. Information subject to the exchange

130. Another aspect of the FHTP's work is to balance the need for greater transparency with not placing too great an administrative burden on tax administrations. As such, a two-step process for exchanging information has been agreed. Under the first step a tax administration provides a summary and some basic information on the ruling. This is done using the template set out at Annex C.[12] Use of a common template streamlines and simplifies the process.

131. The information required to complete the template essentially documents the decision making process that needs to be undertaken by the tax administration that has issued the ruling (i) to determine whether the ruling is covered by the framework; and (ii) to determine with which country it should be exchanged. It does this in a format where entries are largely numeric or use check boxes including drop-down menus if an electronic version is used. It is therefore designed to create minimal extra burden or delay for the issuing tax administration while serving as a useful filter, easily understood in all languages, on the basis of which receiving tax administrations can determine whether to request the ruling itself which would then happen in a second step.

VI. Practical implementation questions

132. The 2014 Progress Report anticipated that the framework set out in that report would apply following the FHTP's 2014 autumn meeting. However, the application of the framework for compulsory spontaneous exchange of information has not yet begun because the inclusion of additional categories of rulings increases the volume of

information that will need to be exchanged. This has therefore required more consideration of the implementation process and the practical implementation issues set out below.

Method of exchange for future rulings – exchange on a regular basis

133. Where a country has provided a ruling that is subject to the obligation to spontaneously exchange it must exchange the relevant information on that ruling with any affected country as quickly as possible and no later than three months after the date on which the ruling becomes available to the competent authority of the country that granted the ruling. Countries must also put in place appropriate systems to ensure that rulings are transmitted to their competent authority without undue delay.

134. However, where a delay is caused by a legal impediment (for example, because of a legal requirement to notify the taxpayer, an appeal filed by the taxpayer against the exchange of information or other judicial procedure), the three month time limit is extended but the relevant country should exchange without undue delay once the legal impediment ceases to exist.

Method of exchange for past rulings

135. Information on past rulings that were issued on or after 1 January 2010 and were still in effect as from 1 January 2014 will also need to be exchanged. This also applies to rulings that have been modified during this period. This process should be completed by the end of 2016.[13] Countries can apply a phased approach to the exchange of past rulings if desired, as long as the exchange of information on rulings is completed by the end of 2016.

VII. Reciprocity

136. There are a number of benefits associated with a reciprocal approach to exchange of information. However, the benefits of reciprocity do not appear to have any relevance where the legal system or administrative practice of only one country provides for a specific procedure. Accordingly, a country that has granted a ruling that is subject to the obligation to spontaneously exchange information cannot invoke the lack of reciprocity as an argument for not spontaneously exchanging information with an affected country, where the affected country does not grant, and therefore cannot exchange, rulings which are subject to the obligation to spontaneously exchange information.[14] This assumes of course that the affected country is committed to applying the framework and to spontaneously exchanging information if it were to grant rulings which would trigger the obligation to spontaneously exchange information.

VIII. Confidentiality of the information exchanged

137. Both the country exchanging information and its taxpayers have a legal right to expect that information exchanged pursuant to the framework remains confidential. The receiving country must therefore have the legal framework necessary to protect information exchanged.

138. All treaties and exchange of information instruments contain provisions regarding tax confidentiality and the obligation to keep information exchanged confidential. Under those provisions, information may only be used for certain specified purposes and

disclosed to certain specified persons. Information exchange partners may suspend or limit the scope of the exchange of information if appropriate safeguards are not in place or if there has been a breach in confidentiality and they are not satisfied that the situation has been appropriately resolved.

139. Domestic laws must be in place in the receiving country to protect confidentiality of tax information, including information exchanged. Effective penalties must apply for unauthorised disclosures of confidential information exchanged.

140. Information exchanged pursuant to this framework may be used only for tax purposes or other purposes permitted by the relevant information exchange instrument. If domestic law allows for a broader use of the information than the applicable instrument, it is expected that international provisions and instruments will prevail over provisions of domestic law.

IX. Best practices[15]

141. The following best practices are intended to reinforce the transparency advancements made in the OECD framework for compulsory spontaneous exchange of information on rulings. They are applicable to both general and taxpayer specific cross-border rulings,[16] except where appropriate distinctions are made between taxpayer-specific rulings, APAs and general rulings. When no distinction is made, the best practices apply to all cross-border rulings which fall within the definition of a ruling set out in this Chapter.[17]

A. Process of granting a ruling

a) Official rules and administrative procedures for rulings should be identified in advance and published, and they should include: (i) the conditions for the applicability of the ruling process; (ii) the grounds for denying a ruling; (iii) the fee structure, if applicable; (iv) the legal consequences of obtaining a ruling; (v) possible sanctions for incomplete or false information provided by a taxpayer; (vi) the conditions for revoking, cancelling or revising a ruling; and (vii) any other guidance that is deemed necessary in order to make the rules sufficiently comprehensive and clear to taxpayers and their advisors.

b) Tax rulings should be issued, and any administrative discretion in granting a ruling should be exercised, only within the limits of, and in accordance with, the country's relevant domestic tax law and administrative procedures, and should be limited to determining how that law and/or any administrative procedures apply to one or more specific operations or transactions intended, planned or undertaken by the taxpayer.

c) Tax rulings should respect applicable international obligations that are incorporated into domestic tax law, for instance, obligations under relevant bilateral treaties.

d) Tax rulings should be issued in writing.

e) Tax rulings should only be issued by the competent government office or authority in charge of this task. Where a ruling is granted by another government office, it should be subject to approval by the competent office.

f) It is recommended that at least two officials are involved in the decision to grant a ruling or there is at least a two-level review process for the decision, in particular in cases where the applicable rules and administrative procedures explicitly refer to discretion or the exercise of judgement by one of the relevant officials.

g) Tax rulings should be binding on the tax authority (to the extent permitted by domestic law[18]), provided that the applicable legislation and administrative procedures and the factual information on which the ruling is based do not change after the ruling has been granted.

h) Taxpayers should apply for a ruling in writing and provide a full description of the underlying operations or transactions for which a ruling is requested. The information should be included in a file supporting the ruling application (the "ruling file"). The ruling file should also include information on the methods and facts for determining the key elements of the tax authority's view (e.g. transfer prices, mark-ups, interest rates, profit margins). There will often be very specific documentation requirements for APAs or other rulings that relate to transfer pricing. Any additional information or relevant facts which are brought to the attention of the tax authority (i.e. in meetings or oral presentations) should be recorded in writing and also be included in the ruling file.

i) Information concerning the applicant (including taxpayer's name, tax residency, tax identification number, commercial register number for corporations and companies) and tax advisor/tax consultant involved should be included in the ruling file and/or the ruling itself.

j) Before taking a decision, the person/s providing the ruling should check that the description of the facts and circumstances is sufficient and justifies the envisaged outcome of the ruling. They should also check that the ruling outcome is consistent with any previous rulings concerning similar legal issues and factual circumstances.

B. Term of the ruling and subsequent audit/checking procedure

a) APAs should only be for a fixed period of time and should be subject to review before being extended.

b) Taxpayers should notify the tax authority about any material changes in the facts or circumstances on which a taxpayer-specific ruling (including an APA) was based, as soon as possible so that the tax administration can assess whether to exchange this information with another country. As part of this notification process, taxpayers should notify tax administrations of any material changes to the related parties with which they transact (for transactions covered by the ruling) and any other changes which would impact on who information should be exchanged with.

c) Effective administrative procedures should be in place to periodically verify that the factual information relied upon and assumptions made when granting taxpayer-specific rulings remain relevant throughout the period of validity of the ruling. This may be particularly necessary in the case of APAs where any underlying assumptions and decisions could be affected by changes in economic circumstances.

d) Rulings should be subject to revision, revocation or cancellation, as the case may be, in the following circumstances:

1. if the taxpayer makes a misrepresentation or omission in applying for the ruling that calls into question the validity of the ruling;
2. if the relevant laws change;
3. if there is a relevant and significant change (i) in the facts or circumstances upon which the ruling was based or (ii) in the validity of the assumptions made.

C. Publication and exchange of information

a) General rulings should be published and made easily accessible to other tax administrations and taxpayers. Ideally, general rulings should be published on the tax administration's website. If not published in full, the website should contain short summaries with links to where the ruling is accessible in full. Also, the published general rulings should be accompanied with a short overview in one of the official languages of the OECD. Publication should take place as soon as it is practicable after the ruling is granted and where possible within six months.

b) For taxpayer-specific rulings, where the ruling issued falls within the scope of the OECD framework for compulsory spontaneous exchange of information on rulings or other applicable commitment to exchange (e.g. under EU law or bilateral treaty), the relevant authority should transmit that ruling to their competent authority without undue delay, in order for that competent authority to exchange information on the ruling with any relevant country as quickly as possible and no later than three months after that in which the ruling becomes available to it (subject to any legal impediments).

Notes

1. For information on the MAC, see: www.oecd.org/tax/exchange-of-tax-information/conventiononmutualadministrativeassistanceintaxmatters.htm.

2. This definition was included in paragraph 161 of the CAN, p. 47, and was also included in 2014 Progress Report, p. 41.

3. In their anonymised or redacted form, such rulings fall within the category of "general rulings", unless they are in fact written in response to a taxpayer-specific ruling request. Of course, in their non-anonymised, non-redacted form, such rulings fall within the category of "taxpayer-specific rulings".

4. APAs may determine the attribution of profit in accordance with Article 7 of the *OECD Model Tax Convention on Income and on Capital: Condensed Version 2014* (OECD Model Tax Convention, OECD, 2014b) as well as transfer pricing between associated enterprises. Such APAs would also fall within the scope of the definition of "ruling" for the purposes of the obligation to spontaneously exchange on rulings.

5. See the definition of APA in the first sentence of paragraph 4.123 of the TP Guidelines, p. 168.

6. See paragraph 3 of the Annex to Chapter IV of the TP Guidelines, p. 330.

7. Law and administrative practice includes statutory law (including relevant treaty provisions), case law, regulations, administrative instructions and practice.

8. See Section III of this Chapter.

9. See paragraph 152 of the CAN, p. 45.

10. See paragraph 153 of the CAN, p. 45.

11. Countries that do not currently have the necessary legal framework in place for spontaneous exchange of information on rulings covered in this Chapter will need to put in place such a framework in order to comply with the obligations under Action 5. In such cases the timelines contained in this section are subject to a country's legal framework. This also takes into account the entry into force and effective date of application of provisions of the relevant exchange of information instruments.

12. The OECD will translate the template into an XML schema with related user guide that can be used for larger transfers of templates.

13. Regarding the timelines contained in this section see footnote 11.

14. See OECD Model Tax Convention, paragraph 15.1 of the Commentary on Article 26, p. 427, which sets out the principle in the context of information exchange on request.

15. In order to follow the best practices, changes in domestic legislation or current ruling practice may be required.

16. All references in the best practices section to general rulings mean cross-border general rulings. A ruling will be considered to be a cross-border ruling where it falls within one of the six categories in Table 5.1.

17. See paragraph 95 above which references the definition of a "ruling".

18. Tax rulings may not be binding where a tax authority made a mistake in the interpretation or application of the law, where it has withdrawn its ruling by written notice that has prospective effect only, or where a ruling contravenes countries' international obligations.

Bibliography

European Union (2011), *Council Directive 2011/16/EU of 15 February 2011*, http://eur-lex.europa.eu/legal-content/EN/TXT/?uri=celex:32011L0016 (accessed 20 July 2015).

OECD (2014a), *Countering Harmful Tax Practices More Effectively, Taking into Account Transparency and Substance*, OECD Publishing, Paris, http://dx.doi.org/10.1787/9789264218970-en.

OECD (2014b), *Model Tax Convention on Income and on Capital: Condensed Version 2014*, OECD Publishing, Paris, http://dx.doi.org/10.1787/mtc_cond-2014-en.

OECD (2010a), *The Multilateral Convention on Mutual Administrative Assistance in Tax Matters Amended by the 2010 Protocol*, OECD Publishing, Paris, http://dx.doi.org/10.1787/9789264115606-en.

OECD (2010b), *OECD Transfer Pricing Guidelines for Multinational Enterprises and Tax Administrations 2010*, OECD Publishing, Paris, http://dx.doi.org/10.1787/tpg-2010-en.

OECD (2004), *Consolidated Application Note: Guidance in Applying the 1998 Report to Preferential Tax Regimes*, OECD, www.oecd.org/ctp/harmful/30901132.pdf.

OECD (2001), *Towards Global Tax Co-operation: Progress in Identifying and Eliminating Harmful Tax Practices*, OECD Publishing, Paris, http://dx.doi.org/10.1787/9789264184541-en.

OECD (1998), *Harmful Tax Competition: An Emerging Global Issue*, OECD Publishing, Paris, http://dx.doi.org/10.1787/9789264162945-en.

Chapter 6

Review of OECD and associate country regimes

I. Introduction

142. The current review of OECD country regimes commenced in late 2010 with the preparation of a preliminary survey of preferential tax regimes in OECD countries, based on publicly available information and without any judgement as to the potential harmfulness of any of the regimes included. Further regimes were subsequently added to the review process based on OECD countries' self-referrals and referrals by other OECD countries.

143. Each OECD country was requested to provide a description of its regimes, along with a self-review using a standard template. The self-reviews were followed by extensive analysis and peer reviews. The reviews were based on the principles and factors set out in the 1998 Report (OECD, 1998) and, where necessary, relevant economic considerations. With the adoption of the BEPS Action Plan (OECD, 2013), G20 countries joined the OECD countries on an equal footing in the FHTP work. The reviews were extended to cover both OECD and associate countries and advanced as follows:

- IP regimes: As all the IP regimes of both OECD and associate countries have been considered together, they have been considered not only in light of the factors as previously applied but also in light of the elaborated substantial activity factor described in Chapter 4 of this Report.
- Non-IP regimes: As the current review commenced before the publication of the BEPS Action Plan, all of the regimes of both OECD and associate countries have been assessed against the factors as previously applied so that there is a consistent approach applied to similar types of regimes such as those for holding companies. With regard to non-IP regimes, the elaborated substantial activity factor has not yet been applied but the FHTP is planning to do this.
- Rulings: FHTP has agreed a framework which will be applied to rulings provided by both OECD and associate countries.

144. Different aspects of the FHTP's work place different requirements on countries in respect of specific regimes. For instance, even if an IP regime is consistent with the nexus approach set out in Chapter 4, a country would still need to exchange any rulings related to that regime under the framework set out in Chapter 5.

II. Conclusions on sub-national regimes and when they are in scope

145. In the course of the current review, the question arose as to whether sub-national regimes offering tax benefits at sub-national level alone are within the scope of the FHTP's work. Given that the no or low effective tax rate gateway factor looks at the

combined effective tax rate for both the national and sub-national levels, a sub-national regime will fall outside the scope of the FHTP's work where the tax rate at the national level or the sub-national level fails to meet the no or low effective tax factor on its own.

146. The 1998 Report does not, however, preclude sub-national regimes from the FHTP's scope of work as a matter of principle, and there is nothing in the history of the FHTP's work precluding sub-national regimes from the scope of its work. In addition, it would be inconsistent with the 1998 Report's broader objective of establishing a "level playing field"[1] to exclude regimes offering tax benefits at the sub-national level alone from the scope of the FHTP's work, particularly where the tax rate at sub-national level represents (or could represent, in the case of a discretionary tax rate) a significant portion of the combined effective tax rate. Bearing this in mind, the FHTP agreed to include sub-national regimes within the scope of its work where both of the following two criteria are satisfied:

a) The national government is ultimately responsible for the general design of the relevant regime and leaves limited discretion to the sub-national government as to whether or not to introduce the regime and/or as to the key features of the regime. The rationale is that in such a case, there is no fundamental difference between the relevant regime and regimes enacted and administered at national level;

b) The tax rate at sub-national level represents (or could represent, in the case of a discretionary tax rate) a significant portion of the combined tax rate and the combined effective tax rate for both the national and sub-national levels meets the no or low effective tax factor.

III. Conclusions reached on regimes reviewed

147. The review process of the FHTP includes the following 43 preferential regimes. The tables below identify the country and the name of the regime and provide the conclusion reached.

Table 6.1 IP regimes

	Country	Regime	Conclusion
1.	Belgium	Patent income deduction	See the paragraph following this table.
2.	People's Republic of China	Reduced rate for high & new tech enterprises	
3.	Colombia	Software regime	
4.	France	Reduced rate for long term capital gains and profits from the licensing of IP rights	
5.	Hungary	IP regime for royalties and capital gains	
6.	Israel	Preferred company regime	
7.	Italy	Patent box	
8.	Luxembourg	Partial exemption for income/gains derived from certain IP rights	
9.	Netherlands	Innovation box	
10.	Portugal	Partial exemption for income from certain intangible property	
11.	Spain	Partial exemption for income from certain intangible assets	
12.	Spain – Basque Country	Partial exemption for income from certain intangible assets	
13.	Spain – Navarra	Partial exemption for income from certain intangible assets	
14.	Switzerland – Canton of Nidwalden	Licence box	
15.	Turkey	Technology development zones	
16.	United Kingdom	Patent box	

148. The IP regimes listed in Table 6.1 were all considered under the criteria in the 1998 Report as well as the elaborated substantial activity factor. Those regimes are inconsistent, either in whole or in part, with the nexus approach as described in this report. This reflects the fact that, unlike other aspects of the work on harmful tax practices, the details of this approach were only finalised in this report while the regimes had been designed at an earlier point in time. Countries with such regimes will now proceed with a review of possible amendments of the relevant features of their regimes.[2] Where no amendments are made, the FHTP will proceed to the next steps in its review process.

Table 6.2 Non-IP regimes

	Country	Regime	Conclusion
17.	Argentina	Promotional regime for software industry	Not harmful
18.	Australia	Conduit foreign income regime	Not harmful
19.	Brazil	PADIS - Semiconductors Industry	Not harmful
20.	Canada	Life insurance business regime	Potentially harmful but not actually harmful
21.	People's Republic of China	Reduced rate for advanced technology service enterprises	Not harmful
22.	Colombia	Foreign portfolio investment regime	Not harmful[3]
23.	Greece	Offshore engineering and construction	Amended
24.	India	Deductions in respect of certain incomes of offshore banking units and international financial services centre	Not harmful
25.	India	Special provisions in respect of newly established units in special economic zones	Not harmful
26.	India	Special provisions relating to income of shipping companies – tonnage tax scheme	Not harmful
27.	India	Taxation of profit and gains of life insurance business	Not harmful
28.	Indonesia	Public/listed company regime	Under review
29.	Indonesia	Investment allowance regime	Under review
30.	Indonesia	Special economic zone regime	Under review
31.	Indonesia	Tax holiday regime	Under review
32.	Japan	Special zones for international competitiveness development	Not harmful[4]
33.	Japan	Measures for the promotion of research and development	Not harmful[5]
34.	Latvia	Shipping taxation regime	Not harmful
35.	Luxembourg	Private asset management company (Société de gestion de patrimoine familial)	Not harmful[6]
36.	Luxembourg	Investment company in risk capital (Société d'investissement en capital à risque) regime	Not harmful[7]
37.	South Africa	Headquarter company	Potentially harmful but not actually harmful
38.	South Africa	Exemption of income in respect of ships used in international shipping	Not harmful
39.	Switzerland – Cantonal level	Auxiliary company regime (previously referred to as domiciliary company regime)	In the process of being eliminated[8]
40.	Switzerland – Cantonal level	Mixed company regime	In the process of being eliminated[9]
41.	Switzerland – Cantonal level	Holding company regime	In the process of being eliminated[10]
42.	Switzerland – Federal level	Commissionaire ruling regime	In the process of being eliminated[11]
43.	Turkey	Shipping regime	Not harmful[12]

149. This Report also establishes the meaning of substantial activities in the context of non-IP regimes, but as mentioned above this analysis has not yet been applied to the regimes. The FHTP will carry out further work to consider in which instances it may be necessary to revisit regimes in light of the agreed substantial activity factor as it applies to non-IP regimes.

IV. Regimes relating to disadvantaged areas

150. Certain countries (e.g. Switzerland[13] and Latvia[14]) have introduced tax incentive regimes designed to encourage development in disadvantaged areas. Whilst they do not specifically provide a preferential treatment for income from IP, they may include (or do not specifically exclude) such income. The FHTP has considered that those regimes, provided they meet certain conditions, do not pose a high risk of BEPS but should be monitored. These regimes will not be further reviewed unless there is an indication of adverse economic effects. To be considered as such a low risk regime applying to disadvantaged areas, the following cumulative conditions would need to be met: (i) the preferential tax treatment is only applicable to a relatively small area (in terms of surface and/or population) selected by reference to the low level structural, economic and social development in the region relative to the country as a whole; (ii) the regime is mainly designed to create new jobs and attract tangible investments and has not been designed to attract IP income or other mobile income; (iii) an entity has to meet significant substance requirements in order to access the preferential tax treatment (e.g. it has to show the generation of new employment, assets and investments); and (iv) the country agrees to keep relevant data (such as the number of entities benefiting from the regime, their sector of activity and the aggregated amount of exempted income) to allow monitoring of the impact of the regime as relevant under the FHTP criteria.

V. Downward adjustments

151. The FHTP considered informal capital and excess profit regimes. The FHTP agreed that a lack of transparency was the main concern with such regimes. It was therefore agreed that in addition to exchanging information on rulings for downward adjustments, information should also be exchanged on downward adjustments where there is no ruling issued. On this basis, the FHTP considered that at this time, it was not necessary to further review these regimes, but that it would be appropriate to monitor the impact of the exchange of information.

Notes

1. See paragraph 8 of the 1998 Report, pp. 8-9.
2. Given its particular features the Chinese regime for High and New Technology will often be more restrictive than the nexus approach and there are only limited circumstances in which income may benefit in excess of the amount computed under the nexus approach.
3. This conclusion was reached by the FHTP without reaching any conclusion that Colombia's regime was within the scope of the work of the FHTP.
4. This regime was considered prior to the approval of the BEPS Action Plan.
5. See footnote 4.
6. See footnote 4.
7. This conclusion was reached by the FHTP without reaching any conclusion that Luxembourg's regime was within the scope of the work of the FHTP.
8. On 5 June 2015, the Swiss Government has submitted a bill for approval in Parliament, wherein it has proposed to abolish the regime (as well as the following three regimes). Subject to the Swiss parliamentary/constitutional approval process, the intention is for the new Federal legislation to be completed by 1 January 2017, followed by a two-year period for the 26 Cantons to revise their laws accordingly.
9. See footnote 8.
10. See footnote 8.
11. See footnote 8.
12. See footnote 4.
13. Swiss relief for newly established or re-designed enterprises.
14. Latvia taxation regime related with the taxpayers investments in special economic zones and free ports (Special economic zones).

Bibliography

OECD (2013), *Action Plan on Base Erosion and Profit Shifting*, OECD Publishing, Paris, http://dx.doi.org/10.1787/9789264202719-en.

OECD (1998), *Harmful Tax Competition: An Emerging Global Issue*, OECD Publishing, Paris, http://dx.doi.org/10.1787/9789264162945-en.

Chapter 7

Further work of the FHTP

152. This Chapter sets out the next steps in the work of the FHTP. The next steps fall into three broad categories: (i) the ongoing work, including monitoring of preferential regimes and the application of the agreed transparency framework, (ii) further development of a strategy to expand participation to third countries, and (iii) considerations of revisions or additions to the existing FHTP criteria.

I. Ongoing work including monitoring

153. Chapters 4 and 5 respectively set out the application of the substantial activities analysis to preferential regimes and the framework for enhanced transparency on rulings. The next steps in this area will include the following.

- IP regimes: The FHTP will monitor preferential IP regimes, and countries should update the FHTP on the legislative progress made in respect of changes to their existing legislation. Existing IP regimes listed in Table 6.1 in Chapter 6 must be amended to comply with the nexus approach (and, if jurisdictions choose to benefit from grandfathering, to comply with the safeguards related to grandfathering and new entrants set out in Chapter 4). Future monitoring will consider any such amendments, and, where no amendments are made to existing IP regimes, the FHTP will move to the next stage of the review process. Chapter 4 provides that, in certain circumstances, countries may permit the use of the nexus ratio as a rebuttable presumption. In these circumstances, certain forms of enhanced transparency and monitoring, set out in Chapter 4, will become applicable, and the FHTP will monitor the implementation and application of the requirements set out in that Chapter. Jurisdictions must also inform the FHTP if they provide benefits under their IP regimes to the third category of IP assets set out in Chapter 4. Finally, Chapter 6 recognises that some regimes designed to promote development in disadvantaged areas will need to be monitored and that countries will be required to keep data on the companies benefitting from those regimes.

- Non-IP regimes: The FHTP will monitor preferential non-IP regimes, noting also that to date the substantial activity factor has only been applied to IP regimes. If countries have concerns about substantial activities in other preferential regimes, these will also need to be reviewed under the elaborated substantial activity factor.

- Transparency Framework: Chapter 5 provides a framework for improving transparency in relation to rulings. Information on future rulings should start to be exchanged from 1 April 2016 and countries have until the end of 2016 to exchange information on past rulings.[1] An ongoing monitoring and review mechanism will be put in place to ensure countries' compliance with the obligation to spontaneously exchange information under the framework. This will involve an annual review by the FHTP starting at the beginning of 2017. As part of that process the FHTP will also evaluate the effectiveness of the framework and whether the scope of the rulings covered, and the information provided by tax administrations, appropriately balances the need to identify BEPS risks with the administrative burden for the sending and receiving jurisdictions. As part of the review process countries that provide taxpayer-specific rulings that fall within the framework will be expected to provide statistical information that includes the following: (i) the total number of spontaneous exchanges sent under the framework, (ii) the number of spontaneous exchanges sent by category of ruling, and (iii) for each exchange, which country or countries information was exchanged with. Countries should also provide details of the cases where they had insufficient information to identify all the countries that they needed to exchange with and therefore applied a best efforts approach. This information should be broken down by category of ruling and should include a brief description of the efforts undertaken to identify relevant related parties.

II. Development of a strategy to expand participation to third countries

154. The need for global solutions to shared challenges is at the heart of the BEPS Project. For this reason, all OECD and G20 countries have worked on an equal footing with the direct participation of an increasing number of developing countries. Action 5 of the BEPS Action Plan (OECD, 2013) explicitly recognised the need to involve third countries and requested the FHTP to develop a strategy to engage non-OECD/ non-G20 countries into the work on harmful tax practices. This is needed to ensure a level playing field and avoid the risk of harmful tax practices being simply displaced to third countries, but also entails involvement and engagement with third countries whether they have preferential regimes or they are otherwise concerned with the work. Against this backdrop the FHTP agreed on the following elements of an engagement strategy with third countries:

- The FHTP's engagement should include third countries that have preferential regimes, as well as other countries that have a stake in the work.
- As part of the engagement, the FHTP will communicate the purpose and objectives of its work also setting out the level of involvement and participation of third countries.
- Additional work will be carried out to implement the engagement strategy in 2016 in the context of the wider objective of designing a more inclusive framework to support and monitor the implementation of the BEPS measures.

III. Consideration of revisions or additions to the existing FHTP criteria

155. The current framework for considering preferential regimes is described in Chapter 3 and uses four key factors and eight other factors to determine whether a preferential regime is potentially harmful. Two of the existing factors (transparency and substantial activity) have already been elaborated as a result of the work on the first output of Action 5. The OECD and G20 countries involved in the FHTP therefore consider that it is too early to accurately identify areas in which the existing criteria might fall short because the impact of the work on substance and transparency cannot yet be

fully evaluated. In addition the benefits of involving third countries in this aspect of the work are recognised.

156. Nevertheless, some areas have been identified as ones that could benefit from further consideration once the FHTP is better able to identify the impact of the other outputs considered in this report. These include the fifth factor set out in the 1998 Report (OECD, 1998) and the application of the ring-fencing factor.

157. The fifth factor which can assist in identifying harmful preferential regimes is "an artificial definition of the tax base." This recognises that rather than offering a preferential tax rate a country can attract mobile income by having a narrow definition of the tax base that subjects less income to tax. This can be achieved, for example, by exempting certain categories of income or by allowing deductions for expenses that are deemed to have been incurred. The 1998 Report notes that such measures may also suffer from a lack of transparency. Some countries have suggested that this factor could also be elevated in importance, as has been done with the twelfth factor; however, the transparency framework set out in Chapter 5 may address many of the transparency concerns raised by such regimes.

158. Ring-fencing is one of the key factors in the 1998 Report and it applies (i) where a regime implicitly or explicitly excludes resident taxpayers from taking advantage of its benefits or (ii) where an entity that benefits from the regime is explicitly or implicitly prohibited from operating in the domestic market. Further guidance on the application of the ring-fencing factor is contained in the CAN (OECD, 2004), which envisages that the ring-fencing factor could apply where the tax result for a wholly domestic transaction is in practice different from that arising for a cross border transaction. In this context it has been suggested that the application of the ring-fencing factor to such scenarios could be made clearer.

Note

1. Countries that do not currently have the necessary legal framework in place for spontaneous exchange of information on rulings covered in Chapter 5 will need to put in place such a framework in order to comply with the obligations under Action 5. In such cases the timelines for spontaneous exchange of information on rulings will be subject to a country's legal framework. This also takes into account the entry into force and effective date of application of provisions of the relevant exchange of information instruments.

Bibliography

OECD (2013), *Action Plan on Base Erosion and Profit Shifting*, OECD Publishing, Paris, http://dx.doi.org/10.1787/9789264202719-en.

OECD (2004), *Consolidated Application Note: Guidance in Applying the 1998 Report to Preferential Tax Regimes*, OECD, www.oecd.org/ctp/harmful/30901132.pdf.

OECD (1998), *Harmful Tax Competition: An Emerging Global Issue*, OECD Publishing, Paris, http://dx.doi.org/10.1787/9789264162945-en.

Annex A

Example of a transitional measure for tracking and tracing

1. Country P implements an IP regime in 2016 that requires tracking and tracing. Taxpayer Q is a technology company that sells products which use multiple IP assets that Taxpayer Q has developed. Prior to 2016, Taxpayer Q did not track and trace either expenditures or income to individual IP assets or products, but Taxpayer Q does have information on the overall R&D expenditures that Taxpayer Q itself incurred, as well as its overall expenditures for related party outsourcing and its overall acquisition costs for 2014 and 2015. Taxpayer Q can then track and trace to product families starting in 2016. Taxpayer Q's expenditures are listed below:

Table A.1 Taxpayer Q's expenditures

2014	All qualifying expenditures (i.e. all R&D expenditures incurred by Taxpayer Q): 5 000 All overall expenditures (i.e. all R&D expenditures incurred by Taxpayer Q, all expenditures for related party outsourcing, and all acquisition costs): 10 000
2015	All qualifying expenditures: 3 000 All overall expenditures: 3 000
2016	All qualifying expenditures: 2 000 Qualifying expenditures for Product Family A: 400 Qualifying expenditures for Product Family B: 1 600 All overall expenditures: 5 000 Overall expenditures for Product Family A: 2 400 Overall expenditures for Product Family B: 2 600
2017	All qualifying expenditures: 2 000 Qualifying expenditures for Product Family A: 1 300 Qualifying expenditures for Product Family B: 700 All overall expenditures: 3 000 Overall expenditures for Product Family A: 2 000 Overall expenditures for Product Family B: 1 000
2018	Qualifying expenditures for Product Family A: 800 Qualifying expenditures for Product Family B: 200 Overall expenditures for Product Family A: 800 Overall expenditures for Product Family B: 800

2. If Country P allows the use of a three-year "average" as a transitional measure, the nexus ratio would be calculated as follows. In 2016, Taxpayer Q therefore calculates the nexus ratio using the average of all of its R&D expenditures over three years. The ratio for 2016 would be 10 000/18 000 before applying the up-lift. For purposes of calculating the three-year average, this ratio does not include any expenditures incurred

before 2014, even if the R&D to create IP Asset Q began before that time, and it uses all expenditures because Taxpayer Q had not yet begun tracking and tracing to product families in 2016. At the same time, Taxpayer Q starts tracking and tracing the expenditures incurred to continue developing IP Asset Q. In 2017, Taxpayer Q would again calculate the nexus ratio using the average of *all* of its R&D expenditures because it did not yet have three years of expenditures tracked to product families. The ratio for 2017 would be 7 000/11 000 before applying the up-lift. In 2018 and all following years, Taxpayer Q would transition to a cumulative approach using expenditures for product families since it would now have three years of expenditures that were tracked by product family. The ratio for Product Family A in 2018 would therefore be 2 500/5 200 before applying the up-lift, and all subsequent qualifying and overall expenditures for Product Family A will be added to that ratio in future years. The ratio for Product Family B in 2018 would be 2 500/4 400 before applying the up-lift, and all subsequent qualifying and overall expenditures for Product Family B will be added to that ratio in future years.

3. This Annex provides only one example of how a transitional measure could be designed to ensure that taxpayers had sufficient time to adapt to tracking and tracing requirements while still complying with the general principles of the nexus approach. Country P could, for example, allow the use of a five-year "average", which would then permit Taxpayer Q to calculate the nexus ratio based on all qualifying and overall expenditures in 2019 and 2020 as well as in 2016, 2017, and 2018.

Annex B Spontaneous exchange on taxpayer-specific rulings under the framework

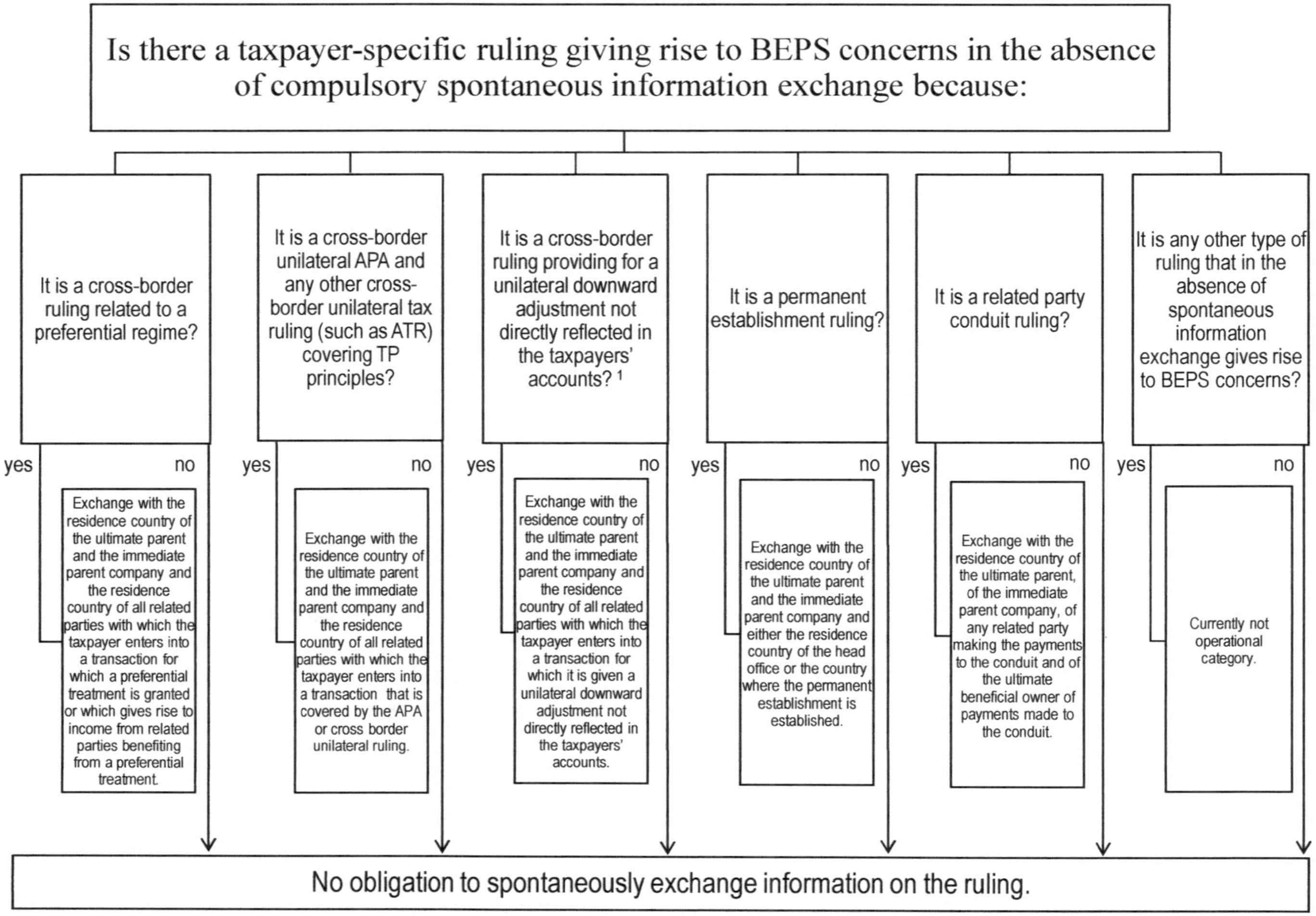

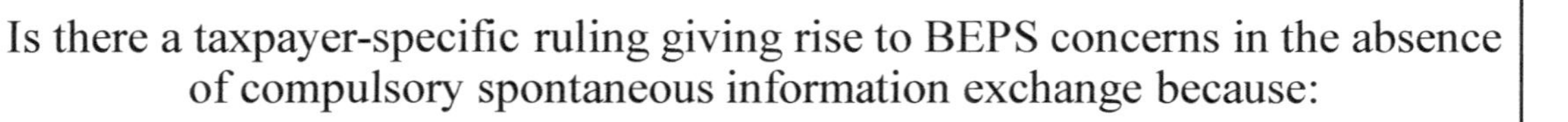

Is there a taxpayer-specific ruling giving rise to BEPS concerns in the absence of compulsory spontaneous information exchange because:

1. It is a cross-border ruling related to a preferential regime?
   - yes: Exchange with the residence country of the ultimate parent and the immediate parent company and the residence country of all related parties with which the taxpayer enters into a transaction for which a preferential treatment is granted or which gives rise to income from related parties benefiting from a preferential treatment.
   - no: No obligation to spontaneously exchange information on the ruling.
2. It is a cross-border unilateral APA and any other cross-border unilateral tax ruling (such as ATR) covering TP principles?
   - yes: Exchange with the residence country of the ultimate parent and the immediate parent company and the residence country of all related parties with which the taxpayer enters into a transaction that is covered by the APA or cross border unilateral ruling.
   - no: No obligation to spontaneously exchange information on the ruling.
3. It is a cross-border ruling providing for a unilateral downward adjustment not directly reflected in the taxpayers' accounts? 1
   - yes: Exchange with the residence country of the ultimate parent and the immediate parent company and the residence country of all related parties with which the taxpayer enters into a transaction for which it is given a unilateral downward adjustment not directly reflected in the taxpayers' accounts.
   - no: No obligation to spontaneously exchange information on the ruling.
4. It is a permanent establishment ruling?
   - yes: Exchange with the residence country of the ultimate parent and the immediate parent company and either the residence country of the head office or the country where the permanent establishment is established.
   - no: No obligation to spontaneously exchange information on the ruling.
5. It is a related party conduit ruling?
   - yes: Exchange with the residence country of the ultimate parent, of the immediate parent company, of any related party making the payments to the conduit and of the ultimate beneficial owner of payments made to the conduit.
   - no: No obligation to spontaneously exchange information on the ruling.
6. It is any other type of ruling that in the absence of spontaneous information exchange gives rise to BEPS concerns?
   - yes: Currently not operational category.
   - no: No obligation to spontaneously exchange information on the ruling.

1. As explained in paragraph 115, it has been agreed that in certain circumstances information will be provided to other relevant tax authorities even where there is no ruling.

Annex C

Template and instruction sheet for information exchange

All fields are mandatory unless otherwise indicated.

1. Ruling reference number, if any.

2. Identification of the taxpayer and where appropriate the group of companies to which it belongs.

Taxpayer identification number (TIN) or other tax reference number		
Legal name of the entity		
Address	Street	
	Building (optional)	
	Suite (optional)	
	Floor (optional)	
	District Name (optional)	
	Post Office Box (optional)	
	Post Code	
	City	
	Country	
	State/Province/Canton (optional)	
Taxpayer's main business activity (optional)		
Name of multinational enterprise (MNE) group, if different		

3. Date of issuance.

4. Accounting periods/tax years covered by the ruling.

5. Type of ruling issued. Please check the appropriate box.

Relating to preferential regime	☐
Unilateral advance pricing arrangement (APA) or other transfer pricing (TP) ruling	☐
Downward adjustment ruling	☐
Permanent establishment (PE) ruling	☐
Conduit ruling	☐

6. Additional information regarding the ruling and the taxpayer (optional).

Transaction amount, if any	
Entity's annual turnover	
Profit of the entity	

7. Short summary of the issue covered by the ruling ideally provided in one of the official languages of the Organisation for Economic Co-operation and Development (OECD) or other language bilaterally agreed. Where this is not possible this can be provided in the native language of the sending jurisdiction.

8. Reason for exchange with the recipient jurisdiction.

Ultimate parent	☐
Immediate parent	☐
Related party with which the taxpayer enters into a transaction for which a preferential treatment is granted or which gives rise to income benefiting from a preferential treatment	☐
Related party with whom the taxpayer enters into a transaction covered by the ruling	☐
Related party making payments to a conduit (directly or indirectly)	☐
Ultimate beneficial owner of income from a conduit arrangement	☐
Head office of permanent establishment (PE) country	☐

9. Details of the entities in the recipient jurisdiction.

	Name of entity	Address	TIN or other tax reference number, where available
1.			
2.			
3.			
...			

Instruction Sheet for the Template on Exchange of Information on Rulings

All fields are mandatory unless otherwise indicated.

1. Ruling reference number, if any.

The ruling reference number should be provided, if it is available.

2. Identification of the taxpayer and where appropriate the group of companies to which it belongs.

This box includes all the information necessary to identify the taxpayer and determine its association with a multinational enterprise (MNE) group. In line with the "Organisation Party" block from the Common Reporting Standard (CRS) the following fields are required: ***taxpayer identification number (TIN) or other tax reference number***, ***legal name of the entity*** (i.e. name of the taxpayer), and ***address.*** Within the address field only the "street", "post code", "city" and "country" where the taxpayer is registered are mandatory fields.

Taxpayer's main business activity field is optional and intended to be a drop-down menu with a list of predefined industry sector codes when used in an application that allows for such functionality.

Name of MNE group, if different aims to provide information on the association of the taxpayer with the MNE group to which it belongs. In some cases the name of the subsidiary may differ from the name of the MNE group making it more difficult to identify the connection between the taxpayer and the MNE group.

3. Date of issuance.

The date on which the ruling was issued is to be inserted in the box. This will generally be the date shown on the ruling or in certain countries where the ruling is held by the tax administrations, it could be the date provided on any written confirmation given to the taxpayer.

4. Accounting periods/tax years covered by the ruling.

This box may have a drop-down menu with the accounting periods/tax years covered by the ruling.

5. Type of ruling given.

These boxes identify the type of ruling that needs to be exchanged. All relevant boxes should be ticked so if a ruling combines several different elements, for instance, a unilateral advance pricing arrangement (APA) and an agreement on the tax treatment of a permanent establishment (PE), then both boxes should be ticked.

6. Further information on the ruling and taxpayer.

These boxes are intended to provide some form of materiality filter to help tax administrations decide if they want to include further information. These boxes are optional, therefore there is no obligation to obtain such information.

Transaction amount is the monetary value of the transaction. The entity's annual turnover is the volume of business of an enterprise as contained in the profits and loss account. It is usually measured by reference to gross receipts, or gross amounts due, from the sale of goods or services by the entity. The profit of the entity is net profit reflecting the difference between gross receipts from business transactions and deductible business expenses.

Where Box 6 of the template is completed this should include the latest figures available from either the rulings file or the taxpayer file and should specify the currency, which should be the currency used in any document made available to the tax administration when it issued the ruling. For example, the transaction amount would be the latest figure for a specific transaction that is covered by the ruling.

7. Short summary of the issue covered by the ruling.

In this box the tax administration should provide a short summary of the issue covered in the ruling and should include a description of the transaction or activity covered by the ruling and any other information that could help the receiving tax administration risk-assess the potential base erosion and profit shifting (BEPS) risks posed by the ruling. For example, in the case of a unilateral APA the summary could set out the type of transaction or income covered and the transfer pricing methodology agreed. As the summary is intended to be high-level it should not generally include details of specific provisions in a country's tax code. The information in the box should ideally be written in one of the official languages of the Organisation for Economic Co-operation and Development (OECD) or other language bilaterally agreed. Where this is not possible this can be provided in the native language of the sending jurisdiction.

8. Reason for exchange with the recipient jurisdiction.

The information provided in this field will tell the recipient jurisdiction why it is receiving the ruling. The recipient jurisdiction must be one of the relevant jurisdictions under the framework. The precise reason for the exchange will be indicated by the box ticked.

9. Details of the entities in the recipient jurisdiction.

This box provides further information on any entities to which the ruling relates and that are resident in the recipient jurisdiction. There is the ability to identify more than one entity where a ruling relates to more than one entity in that jurisdiction. The ***name of the entity*** and the ***address*** are mandatory and the ***TIN or other tax reference number*** should be provided where such information is available.

ORGANISATION FOR ECONOMIC CO-OPERATION AND DEVELOPMENT

The OECD is a unique forum where governments work together to address the economic, social and environmental challenges of globalisation. The OECD is also at the forefront of efforts to understand and to help governments respond to new developments and concerns, such as corporate governance, the information economy and the challenges of an ageing population. The Organisation provides a setting where governments can compare policy experiences, seek answers to common problems, identify good practice and work to co-ordinate domestic and international policies.

The OECD member countries are: Australia, Austria, Belgium, Canada, Chile, the Czech Republic, Denmark, Estonia, Finland, France, Germany, Greece, Hungary, Iceland, Ireland, Israel, Italy, Japan, Korea, Luxembourg, Mexico, the Netherlands, New Zealand, Norway, Poland, Portugal, the Slovak Republic, Slovenia, Spain, Sweden, Switzerland, Turkey, the United Kingdom and the United States. The European Union takes part in the work of the OECD.

OECD Publishing disseminates widely the results of the Organisation's statistics gathering and research on economic, social and environmental issues, as well as the conventions, guidelines and standards agreed by its members.

OECD PUBLISHING, 2, rue André-Pascal, 75775 PARIS CEDEX 16
(23 2015 32 1 P) ISBN 978-92-64-24118-3 – 2015-01

www.ingramcontent.com/pod-product-compliance
Lightning Source LLC
LaVergne TN
LVHW081420110826
845149LV00010B/1816

* 9 7 8 9 2 6 4 2 4 1 1 8 3 *